NO LONGER TWO BUT ONE

Powerful Spiritual Principles
From the Word
on Marriage, Divorce and Remarriage

by
Darrell Huffman

Harrison House
Tulsa, Oklahoma

No Longer Two But One –
Powerful Spiritual Principles From the Word
on Marriage, Divorce and Remarriage
ISBN 0-89274-997-0
Copyright © 1997 by Darrell Huffman
Huffman New Life Victory Center
1101 Cedar Crest Drive
Huntington, West Virginia 25705

Published by Harrison House, Inc.
P. O. Box 35035
Tulsa, Oklahoma 74153

Contents

Introduction

In our study of marriage, divorce and remarriage, we will begin with the subject of marriage, though many people would want to start off with divorce and then go to remarriage.

So, you might ask, *why deal with marriage first?*

Because you really need to know what marriage is all about before you will know what divorce is.

Apparently, the divorced person doesn't really understand the marriage covenant which he/she entered, so that person shouldn't be going back into marriage again until learning a few things about it. Why make the same mistakes over and over and over?

Besides that, most people don't know who is supposed to do what, or how, or when with regard to marriage and divorce. They don't know what is legal and what is illegal.

Unfortunately in most cases, it seems the Church has taken everything having to do with these subjects, jumbled them all together in a bag, shaken them really well, then poured them out, saying, "Whatever way they fall, that's just the way it is." But that is a big mistake.

We really need to study about marriage, divorce and remarriage because these days far too many Christians are being divorced.

Several years ago, when studying the subject of divorce, we found that about fifty percent of couples in the secular world and about one out of three Christian couples were divorcing. So believers weren't far behind unbelievers when it came to this problem area. And the divorce rate has continued to increase.

The trouble is, the responsibility of teaching on marriage and family has shifted from being the responsibility of the church to that of the school system, or the politicians, or the social workers. But teaching on this subject is supposed to come from the Bible. We should be finding out from God's Word how marriage is to be organized.

For answers to questions about marriage, divorce and remarriage, the best place for us to go is the Word of God and the best Person to draw from is the Lord Jesus Christ. We will be learning some answers from the Lord Himself, because He is the Word. (John 1:1,14.)

As Jesus said in John 8:32, **And ye shall know the truth, and the truth shall make you free**. You cannot be free in any area of life until you receive the Word of God, which is the Truth.

The apostle John wrote in Third John, verse 2, **Beloved, I wish above all things that thou mayest prosper and be in health, even as thy soul prospereth**. To prosper and succeed in life, you must renew your mind to the laws of God — the Truth. If you don't know the Truth, you will be kept in bondage.

Now you might say, "Well, if I don't know it, then it won't hurt me."

But in Hosea 4:6 God says, **My people are destroyed for lack of knowledge**.

If you don't know what the Word of God says, you will be held captive to the world's system and be cut off from the blessings of God. But when you come to know the Word and begin to walk in it, you will be set free from that bondage. The moment you receive the Truth into your heart and let it become real to you, then you will be walking in the blessings of God. That's God's Word on it!

Let's go now into the Scriptures and find out what there is to learn on the subjects of marriage, divorce and remarriage.

CHAPTER 1

What Is Marriage?

Our basic Scripture text in this study is taken from Matthew, chapter 19.

> **And it came to pass, that when Jesus**
> **had finished these sayings, he departed**
> **from Galilee, and came into the coasts of**
> **Judaea beyond Jordan;**
>
> **And great multitudes followed him;**
> **and he healed them there.**
>
> **Matthew 19:1,2**

Thank God, Jesus healed people and set them free! If you want to be healed and blessed, you have to follow Jesus. You can't be resisting Him and fighting against Him. Notice that verse 2 doesn't say, when Jesus came into the area, great multitudes *debated* Him; it says they *followed* Him.

To follow Jesus means to give up your own direction and go His way. You can't really follow somebody unless you willfully submit to that person and go the way he leads. That's the key to this.

Jesus said, **And these signs shall follow them that believe...** (Mark 16:17). In other words, if you will believe Jesus and follow after His teachings and do what He has told you to do, then you will be healed in every area of your life.

I want you to realize that the words we have read from Matthew, chapter 19, were not just written by coincidence. God had a reason for putting them there.

If you want to get healed or delivered or set free, you have to make up your mind that you will follow the Lord Jesus Christ and obey His Word. You have to make this decision and say: "I'm going to follow the Lord Jesus and Him only. I'm going to take off my religious glasses and quit reading things into the Bible. I'm going to receive what Jesus says and just accept it for what it is — the true Word of God."

🍂 🍂 🍂

 # The Pharisees With Their Religious Question

Now notice Matthew 19, verse 3:

The Pharisees also came unto him, tempting him, and saying unto him, Is it lawful for a man to put away (or divorce) **his wife for every cause?**

When you are in a place where the power of God is being poured out, not everybody has come to receive that power.

As we saw in verse 2, there was a great multitude following the Lord Jesus Christ. They came to hear Him and to be healed and to have their needs met.

But right in the middle of that great multitude of people, there appeared a group known as the Pharisees. These were the religious zealots of that day, people who were bound by the legalism of the Law and who followed what the letter of the Law said. They weren't turned on to God; they were just turned on to their religion. They were against the coming of the Messiah and were opposed to all the moves of God. They were living in the past.

They questioned everything and had absolutely no faith. They refused to walk by anything they couldn't understand or reason out in their own minds. Whenever there was a miracle, they had to explain it away or be able to justify why it had happened. They couldn't accept something unless it was laid out for them in black and white. Every *i* had to be dotted and every *t* crossed, with every paragraph being exact in its presentation.

This is a good description of the Pharisees. We have people like that today. They can't believe anything God says unless they can reason it out and draw a picture of it on a piece of paper. The problem is, anyone operating that way will be defeated.

So the Pharisees were not following after Jesus. They didn't come to receive anything from His ministry. They came asking questions that would cause Him some problems.

They Were Tempting Jesus

Again, Matthew 19:3 says:

The Pharisees also came unto him, tempting him....

The *New King James Version* says they were **testing Him**.

You see, the Pharisees didn't come to Jesus with a sincere heart. Being bound up in their religious traditions, they weren't really seeking an answer to their question. They came to Him with a temptation, or test. They didn't agree with Him, so they came to debate Him and to prove their own beliefs in order to get their own religious cause established.

I want you to realize that you can't get an answer from God if you are always questioning everything He does. You can't be debating Him and trying to prove yourself right in His eyes. You can't expect to receive His blessing by proving your own way or your own philosophy. You have to come to Him with an open heart and follow Him, letting Him have His way in your life.

When the Word of God is being preached and the power of God is moving to set people free, those who aren't free have to make a choice: either they accept the Word and get set free, or they reject the Word and stay just the way they are. The ones who reject it and want to stay the same are usually fussing about the Word and are always questioning it.

So the Pharisees came asking Jesus a question when they didn't really care what His answer might be. They didn't want to change; they wanted to stay as they were. They were only tempting Him and testing Him. Again, their question was:

Is it lawful for a man to put away (or divorce) **his wife for every cause?**

In other words, they were asking: "Can we divorce our wives for any reason — if we just don't get along with them or just feel that we want a divorce?"

But their question wasn't really sincere. They were just trying to throw a snare in Jesus' path. Why? Because there was a move of God at work. Every time God is moving, the enemy will come in and try to keep people from allowing the move of God to flow through them.

Jesus said in Mark 10:30 that when the blessings of God come to us in this life, there will be a hundredfold blessing, **with persecutions**; in other words, with temptations, tests and trials. Along with God's blessing, there will always come a little persecution.

🍃 🍃 🍃

Jesus Answered Religion With the Word of God

So the religious ones in Jesus' day came at Him with this question about divorce. Then beginning in verse 4 we find Jesus' answer:

And he answered and said unto them,

Have ye not read...?

Notice that Jesus responded to their question by questioning them. He said, **Have ye not read...?** He was saying:

"Why are you philosophizing about all these things? Why don't you get out the Holy Scriptures and find out what God has to say about it in His Word? I will take you there and show it to you."

Then He took them straight to the Word of God.

Now why did He do that? Because many times the Pharisees didn't quote the Word of God; instead, they were always quoting commentaries about the Word.

That sounds a little bit like the pharisaical person of today, doesn't it? He doesn't want to go back to the Word of God. He doesn't want to go back to God's plan in the beginning and find out what God wants to do about it. Instead, he asks: "But what about *my* seminar training? What about *my* theological education? What about *my* denomination?"

When the Lord was questioned by these religious men about the subject of divorce, He was saying to them:

"Before you start looking at divorce, you have to realize that it wasn't God's intention for anybody to ever get divorced. You need to understand that God put marriage together, and I will tell you what God said about it."

The first thing He did then was to take them back to God's Word on the subject of marriage. If you want to know about marriage and about God's plan for marriage, you have to find out what the Word has to say about it. You can't really get a clear understanding of what divorce is until you have a clear understanding of what marriage is.

So when answering the Pharisees, the Lord didn't deal with their commentaries, or their philosophies, or their religious beliefs. He gave no place to the liberal theologians of His day, and He didn't put up with them for one minute. He didn't debate them about their philosophy. He didn't argue with them over their denominational training. He didn't quarrel with them about what they thought. He said:

"You can't be adding to or taking away from the Law of God. You can't be making your own opinion or following your own philosophy or having your own religious thoughts. What you think doesn't really matter. You have to go back to God's Word and do it the way He says. Your way doesn't count; it's what God's Word says that matters."

Back to the Beginning

And he answered and said unto them, Have ye not read, that he which made them at the beginning made them male and female,

And said, For this cause shall a man leave father and mother, and shall cleave to his wife: and they twain shall be one flesh?

Wherefore they are no more twain (or two), **but one flesh. What therefore God hath joined together, let not man put asunder** (divide, separate).

Matthew 19:4-6

Notice when they asked Jesus about marriage and divorce and remarriage, He took them back to the beginning. Look at verse 4 again. He said to them:

Have ye not read, that he which made them at the beginning made them male and female?

He took them to God's original plan.

You have to find out what the Word says; and it isn't what has happened since the beginning, but what God did in the beginning.

You need to understand this: God's plan and purpose and precepts don't change. Man and civilizations may change, but God never changes. Scripture says:

For I am the Lord, I change not.

Malachi 3:6

> **Jesus Christ the same yesterday, and to day, and for ever.**
>
> **Hebrews 13:8**

Now we may alter God's plan in our own lives, but we cannot alter God's plan. It was God's plan for man to rule and reign on planet Earth. By accepting the devil's trap in the garden, man turned from God and altered that plan for a while. Then God brought Jesus so that man could be set free from the snare of the devil.

Romans 5:17 says that **they which receive abundance of grace and of the gift of righteousness shall reign in life by one, Jesus Christ.** Revelation 1:6 says Jesus Christ **hath made us kings and priests unto God and his Father.** God's plan has been restored.

God never changed His original plan for man. He always wanted fellowship with us. He always had a plan for us, and He always put that plan to work. We may try to alter it sometimes, but God does not change. So we can begin to see some insights into God's plan.

Jesus began to reiterate some of the things God had done, which we can see in Genesis, chapter 2. Jesus was saying: "Didn't you see where He made them male and female in the beginning? Then He joined them together and made them one."

So God is the originator of marriage. He instituted it. He put it together. Therefore, only God has the right to govern it.

The Definition of Marriage

Marriage is a joining together of a man and a woman to become husband and wife. They are no longer two separate individuals; they become one in the eyes of God.

Now does that mean they lose their own identity when they get married? No, it means they take on a partner in life.

God takes the man and begins to mold him into his wife, his partner. He takes the man's partner and begins to mold her into her husband. The two of them, as husband and wife, become one in the spirit and in the flesh; one in purpose, in goals, in dreams, in vision.

They have entered into the miracle of marriage. Two different people with two different personalities come together and become one in the eyes of the Lord. They join together in life to become one in companionship. They commune with one another and work with one another in making life's decisions.

God laid out the institution of marriage so that a man and a woman would join together, have a family and live their entire lives here on earth together. He didn't plan on divorce being an option, and He definitely didn't want divorce resulting just because the husband and wife didn't get along with one another.

Notice here that the Lord, in quoting from the book of Genesis, put a great responsibility on the husband. In Matthew 19, verse 5, Jesus said:

> **For this cause shall a man leave father and mother, and shall cleave to his wife: and they twain shall be one flesh?**

When entering into marriage, the man leaves his father and mother. Why? Because he is expected to provide for his own home, to be the spiritual leader and guide over his wife and family.

According to Genesis, chapter 2, God formed the woman and brought her to the man, and they were joined as husband and wife. The Scripture says the man **shall** *cleave* **to his wife**. What does that mean?

To cleave means "to adhere; cling (to)...to be faithful (to)."[1] In other words it means to join, to make a commitment, to become one with. The husband and wife are to cleave, or draw together, as one. That means a man must take the responsibility of making the marriage work.

In the beginning God instituted and ordained marriage. He established it, set it into motion and laid down the laws regarding it.

Marriage was not a man-made idea, so man cannot alter it or govern it.

God wrote out His plan for marriage, and Jesus was saying, "If you want it governed, you have to go back to God."

Liberal Views of Marriage

Now notice Jesus did not say, "In the beginning God made them male and male, or female and female."

Modern liberal theology seems to be governing the civilization we live in today and allowing homosexual couples, both male and female, to be married in the church. They are altering marriage to fit man's own ideas.

But man does not have the right to do that. The Word says God made them male and female – not male and male, nor female and female. Homosexuality is a sin; God did not ordain it and does not permit it. (Lev. 18:22; 20:13; Rom. 1:26,27.)

There are other ideas going on today regarding marriage, with the husband and wife wanting to do his or her own thing. Many women are maintaining their maiden name when married. Joint bank accounts are no longer the "in thing." The husband has his own career; the wife has her own career. Man does his thing; woman does her thing. There just doesn't seem to be a real sense of two people joining together in marriage.

But again, man does not have the right to alter God's plans.

Now as Scripture says, God joins them together. But in modern times, people have come to think that it's all right for couples to live together. After all, they say, living together is the same as being married.

But it isn't. Remember, to cleave means to join, to make a commitment, to become one. Just living together will not cause what God wants for a man and a woman to take place.

Marriage — A Spiritual Covenant

Notice again in verse 6 Jesus says:

> **Wherefore they are no more twain, but one flesh. What therefore God hath joined together, let not man put asunder.**

Marriage in God's mind is more than just a legal contract between a man and a woman. Those two are not just being joined together by the government or by man's law or by society. It isn't just an emotional or physical attachment that brings them together. Marriage is a *spiritual* covenant.

God set marriage into motion, so only God can put a man and a woman together. They are spiritually joined together in marriage by the hand of God.

So, marriage is God's institution, and God governs it. If

you don't like that idea, then you will have to talk to God. You see, if you really want the truth and want to be set free regarding marriage, you have to find out what God has to say about it.

Again, when Jesus was asked by the Pharisees about divorce, He said, "Go back to the beginning and find out about the laws of God that were laid down."

God is the One Who put marriage into motion, and He is the One Who oversees it.

God puts a man and woman together. They each have to separate themselves from their own families and join themselves together to become a separate entity, forming a family of their own.

God's rule or law governing marriage does not say that a man or woman can stay hooked up to their own mom and dad. They have to cut the umbilical cord that has been holding them to their parents for security, whether it's emotional or financial.

Jesus said, "Let's go back to the beginning." So let's do that now by looking in the book of Genesis and finding out what God said in the beginning.

Chapter 2

Relationship

**And the Lord God formed man of the
dust of the ground, and breathed into his
nostrils the breath of life; and man became
a living soul.**

Genesis 2:7

After God had created man and had been fellowshipping with him for a time, He looked down upon man and saw that he was alone.

A Help Meet for Man

God's verdict for man's single life can be found in verse 18 of Genesis, chapter 2:

And the Lord God said, It is not good

**that the man should be alone; I will make
him an help meet for him.**

There is something we need to see in these two verses
from Genesis, chapter 2: Though Adam was alive and in
daily fellowship with God, there still was a void in his life.
God saw that man needed somebody with whom he could
share his life.

You see, Adam was a living being. God had breathed
spirit into him. So, he already had a spiritual walk with God
and was in fellowship with Him. He was busy about his
Father's business, doing what God told him to do. But then
God said, **It is not good that the man should be alone; I
will make him an help meet for him.**

> **And out of the ground the Lord God
> formed every beast of the field, and every
> fowl of the air; and brought them unto
> Adam to see what he would call them: and
> whatsoever Adam called every living crea-
> ture, that was the name thereof.**
>
> **And Adam gave names to all cattle,
> and to the fowl of the air, and to every**

**beast of the field; but for Adam there was
not found an help meet for him.**

Genesis 2:19,20

Now what is meant by the term *help meet?* It means a
helper, one who is appropriate to, corresponding to and
comparable with.[1]

God didn't say, "Now, Adam, you are really a super-
duper guy, but I'm only going to give you a second-rate
woman." You see, that idea is where we can get into trouble
many times.

God was saying: "I will make him a helper, one who is
comparable to him, who is built on an equal plane with
him. I will bring that helper to him and make them one
flesh together."

So then God created a help meet for man, one who
would work together with him. Let's see this in the
Scriptures:

**And the Lord God caused a deep sleep
to fall upon Adam, and he slept: and he
took one of his ribs, and closed up the
flesh instead thereof;**

And the rib, which the Lord God had taken from man, made he a woman, and brought her unto the man.

And Adam said, This is now bone of my bones, and flesh of my flesh: she shall be called Woman, because she was taken out of Man.

Therefore shall a man leave his father and his mother, and shall cleave unto his wife: and they shall be one flesh.

And they were both naked, the man and his wife, and were not ashamed.

Genesis 2:21-25

Now notice here that God made this help meet out of man, and she was comparable to him. Not less than, but exactly as.

God brought the woman to the man. He put them together in order that they would do what He had called them to do.

❧ ❧ ❧

 # Both Man and Woman Had Dominion Over the Earth

In Genesis, chapter 1, God didn't just delegate His authority to Adam only. He placed both Adam and Eve in a place of authority and gave them dominion over the earth and the works of His hands. I will prove this to you in verses 26 and 27:

> **And God said, Let us make man in our image, after our likeness: and let them have dominion over the fish of the sea, and over the fowl of the air, and over the cattle, and over all the earth, and over every creeping thing that creepeth upon the earth.**
>
> **So God created man in his own image, in the image of God created he him;** *male and female created he them.*

Now look at verse 28:

> **And God blessed them, and God said unto them....**

God said unto *them*. That means He blessed both the male and the female.

How do you know He really was talking to the male and the female?

Because it takes a male and a female to replenish the earth. In verse 28 God said to them:

> **Be fruitful, and multiply, and replenish the earth, and subdue it: and have dominion over the fish of the sea, and over the fowl of the air, and over every living thing that moveth upon the earth.**

God gave the man and woman — the husband and wife — dominion together. They were to rule together, to flow together, to be one together.

First, Relationship With God

I want you to realize something: God did not form the marriage covenant to bring man into fellowship with Himself. The reason for marriage is not to get you saved.

As was mentioned earlier, Adam was already busy about his Father's business. He wasn't out of fellowship with God, moaning and groaning, saying, "If I could just have a wife, I could do something for God."

Adam was already secure in his walk with the Lord. He was operating in faith and was being led by the Spirit of God. His relationship with God had already been set into motion, and he was doing what God had told him to do.

The point I want to make is this: For a man to have a successful marriage, he must first have a successful relationship with the Lord. That's important whether he is entering into marriage for the first time or is getting remarried.

He should not be getting married in order to get close to God. His relationship with God must already be intact, or his marriage will suffer as a result.

Some women say, "Well, if I could just get a husband who would be one with me, then I could get involved with God and really work for Him."

But you don't get married so that you can have a greater spiritual walk with God. In fact, there is no guarantee that the person you marry is going to live for God. (1 Cor. 7:12-14.)

That would be as bad as a husband and wife who don't get along deciding to have a baby because they think their baby will draw them closer together. It won't. The baby will only add more problems.

You see, what makes a marriage really succeed is not the relationship between the husband and the wife, but the relationship they each have with the Lord. You need to understand this: Your relationship must go up to God before it can go out to anybody else.

Where people make a mistake is by thinking that marriage takes preeminence over everything. It does not.

So, remember, before God instituted marriage, He instituted relationship.

If you expect to follow God's laws on marriage, then before you can even be a candidate for marriage, you should be saved, be filled with the Holy Spirit and be living for God.

The best way for you to have a successful marriage is to get busy about the Father's work and be obedient to God. First, develop your relationship with the Lord; then let Him bring the person into your life that you are to marry. You must be serving God with all of your heart and doing what He has told you to do. If your relationship is right with Him, it will carry over into a relationship with your spouse.

 ## The World Offers Plenty of Opportunity To Sin

I remember when my wife, Bonnie, and I had gone to college. While I was playing football, she went for two years to get her associate degree; then we got married. I continued on with college while she went into the work force. That was in the early '70s, and even in those days people's behavior was fairly radical. It seemed that young men and women didn't care whether they were married.

There were plenty of opportunities for me to sin against my wife by having an affair with another woman. Then with Bonnie working in an office with salesmen around her all the time, she found herself in an environment where the men had lots of opportunities to make passes at the women.

But Bonnie and I didn't have to question our loyalty to each other. For me to have committed adultery against her would first have required me to sin against Jesus, and Bonnie felt the same way about cheating on me. I knew she loved the Lord more than she loved going out and getting into sin. I was sure that she would never break the vow she had made in committing herself to God, even before she made her marriage vow to me.

If both you and your spouse have a right relationship with God and are serving the Lord the way you should, trust will automatically be built between the two of you.

I didn't marry Bonnie in order to strengthen my relationship with the Lord. My relationship with Him was already established, and the Lord was working in my life. I got married for the mere reason that I was lonely and wanted a help meet, someone to work with me as I served the Lord.

God's plan is, first of all, that we develop a relationship with Him.

Too many times, people put the flesh before the spirit. They want to receive practical things before they receive spiritual things. They ought to do as Jesus said in Matthew 6:33: **But seek ye first the kingdom of God, and his righteousness; and all these things shall be added unto you.**

You have to put God and His will first in your life, so that your relationship with God will be established.

 # Then Comes the Husband/Wife Relationship

I want you to understand something about the relationship between the husband and the wife. According to First Peter 3:7, we are **heirs together of the grace of life.** Did you know that man did not rule over woman until after the fall? That was part of the curse. God said in Genesis 3:16 that the woman's desire would be toward her husband and that he would rule over her.

But when God first established marriage, He didn't organize it as a way for the macho man to dominate the innocent little woman. He created husband and wife as heirs together in this life. He put His anointing on both of them and made them compatible and comparable with each other.

In the beginning Eve was created to enhance, to strengthen and to bring fullness to Adam. Adam, in turn, was to love, to cherish and to honor her. Working together, they were to rule and reign in this life. They were to flow together as one, complementing each other in everything they did.

You see, God's plan is for a husband and wife to enter into covenant with one another. As was described earlier, marriage is not just a legal contract. It isn't just an agreement written up by lawyers and put on file with the county clerk. Marriage is a covenant that was ordained and instituted by God in the beginning.

God brought man and woman together and made them one. He put the woman on the same plane as the man. God gave her to the man and, as Jesus said in Matthew 19:6, He made the two of them one flesh.

A Covenant of Companionship

Did God bring Eve as a help meet to Adam just so they could have children?

No.

You see, a man and woman don't have to get married to have children. Society has certainly proven that in today's world.

Marriage was not just for sexual purposes, though Hebrews 13:4 says that the marriage bed is undefiled. The sexual part of marriage is a privilege given to the husband and wife. But sex isn't just for making babies. That isn't why marriage was instituted.

So, why did God bring Eve to Adam? Because God saw that it was not good for him to be alone.

How do you get rid of loneliness? By companionship.

So, what is marriage in the sight of God, and why did He bring it into the picture?

Marriage is the joining together of a man and woman and the forming of a covenant of companionship between them as equals. This covenant of companionship, including spirit, soul and body, was formed by God and is to be governed by His laws.

The man and woman come together as husband and wife to fill the void in each other's lives through companionship, thereby ridding themselves of loneliness.

These two, who are heirs of the grace of this life, come together in the love of God to join in the work of God, to be companions with one another through thick and thin, and to flow together as one. They are to walk in the plan of God together and do what God has called them to do.

That's what marriage is — a covenant of companionship.

Marriage Brings a Special Closeness

Notice something now in Genesis, chapter 2, verse 25:

**And they were both naked, the man
and his wife, and were not ashamed.**

I believe this verse is talking about more than just the physical realm. It means the man and the woman became really close to one another and were exposed to one another, showing both their weaknesses and their strengths.

If a husband and wife are operating in the marriage covenant the way God intends, there ought not be any secrets between them. God ordained that they be able to sit down with one another and open themselves to one another. That's why they got married: so they wouldn't be alone.

The husband should be able to share with his wife his heartaches and hurts, as well as his good times and victories.

Even a macho man must be able to open up his heart and share his innermost feelings with his wife. Regardless of any fears or hurts that may have hindered him, he must be able to reveal to her the dark recesses of his life. He shouldn't be ashamed to say to her, "Here's what has caused me problems." He must feel free to be himself.

The wife should be able to come to her husband and share the intimate secrets of her life without being put down or ridiculed. She should be loved and honored by him.

It's a shame that she would have to go to another woman in order to share her heart's desires and to receive support in prayer. Now it's fine for her to have prayer partners, but her husband should be the one who is helping her through that situation.

To the person who is engaged to be married, I would say this: While you are going through the engagement period, just be yourself. Somewhere down the line, you will have to show yourself the way you really are. It would be impossible for you to keep on faking it year after year. You won't be able to keep up your guard forever.

So, get to know the person you are planning to marry. Then after you are married, stay open to one another, and the two of you will be able to flow together.

Remember, your relationship must first be toward God, then you can have a true relationship with your partner for life.

The two of you are to come together in marriage — that covenant of companionship — full of love and anointed of God. Depend first on God; then on one another.

You are to separate yourselves from your own families and take on your responsibilities as heirs of the grace of this life together.

You are to open up your hearts to one another, sharing both the good times and the bad times.

As long as the two of you are looking to God and trusting Him with all your heart, you will get the job done. That's relationship.

CHAPTER 3

Divine Order Established

As we have pointed out, man and woman are equal in God's eyes. There is neither male nor female in the sight of God; both are heirs together of the grace of this life. (Gal. 3:28; 1 Peter 3:7.)

But according to divine order, who in the marriage will be making the decisions? Let me show you about having divine order in the home.

The Husband Is Head of the House

Genesis 2, verse 7, says that when God made man, **man became a living soul**; and in verse 18 God said, **I will make him an help meet for him.**

Then verse 22 says:

**And the rib, which the Lord God had
taken from man, made he a woman, and
brought her unto the man.**

I want you to notice in this verse that it says God
brought the woman to the man. There was to be order in
the home.

In Ephesians, chapter 5, the apostle Paul writes about
what the Lord had taught him on this subject. In verse 23
he says that the husband is the head of the wife:

**For the husband is the head of the
wife, even as Christ is the head of the
church: and he is the saviour of the body.**

In God's plan for the marriage, He has given responsibility to the husband to take the lead in the home. The husband is to be an example before his wife and his children,
as well as to all who enter his house.

The Wife Submits to Her Husband

God has given the wife responsibility to submit to her
husband and to help him.

Some women might disagree with me and say: "I just knew he was a woman hater! After saying all those good things about how women are heirs together with men, then he turned around and put us back under man's authority."

But I'm not a woman hater.

Here is the thing you need to understand: God brought the woman to the man and called her man's help meet. She was to be a helper, one who was comparable to him. Now I didn't make this up; that's what God says in His Word. Remember, we went back to the beginning and read it from Genesis, chapter 2.

Ephesians, chapter 5, describes the wife as one who is subordinate, who will submit herself to her husband and join herself to him. Now this doesn't mean she becomes less of a person. It means she begins to mold herself to him and work together with him. That's God's description of marriage.

Now a woman may say: "But it just isn't fair for me to have to mold myself to my husband and hook up with him and submit to him. I don't want to do that."

Then I would respond: "Well, if your husband isn't the person you want to mold to and submit to and hook up with, then why did you marry him in the first place?"

Now we can see how divorce takes place.

Do you know why marriage is under such attack today? Because Satan knows that if he could destroy the home, he could destroy the Church. If he could destroy the Church, he could destroy society. Then he would be able to rule and to reign over God's people.

The Husband and Wife Are To Be One

First Peter 3:7 says the husband is to dwell with his wife according to knowledge and to treat her as the weaker vessel. The problem is, most husbands these days have no idea how they are to dwell with their wives.

He says to her: "Fix breakfast. Bathe the kids and take them to school. Clean the house. Feed the dog. Wash the car. Mow the grass. And where's my supper? You don't do anything all day, woman!"

No wonder there are such problems between men and women. As long as they are living without God, it's difficult for their marriage to work.

The husband is supposed to love his wife and be watching out for her, overseeing her and protecting her. That doesn't mean he can dominate her and dictate to her and stifle her growth. He must care for her and minister to her. Then it will be pleasing to him when she succeeds in life.

In Ephesians, chapter 5, you will find that the woman is doubly blessed because the Lord is her spiritual head and, when she marries, her husband becomes her domestic head. Then she will have a twofold protection.

So, you see, God has said the husband and wife are to come together and become one flesh. The husband is to provide and oversee and work with his wife and be her spiritual leader. The wife is to help her husband by subordinating herself to him, working with him and showing him reverence and respect. Then the two of them will be walking together under God's plan for marriage.

Now we know God took one of Adam's bones to form the woman; but He didn't take one of his toe bones, or a piece of his cranial cavity, or a portion of his spine. If God had formed her out of Adam's foot, man would be able to put woman under his foot and just keep her there! If she had been brought out of Adam's skull, then woman could be henpecking man all the time. If she had been taken out of Adam's back, man could force woman to always be walking three paces behind him.

But God brought the woman out of man's rib, which is in his side. Why? Because they are heirs together. That means the husband is to reach out and put his arm around his wife. He is to protect her and care for her and strengthen her.

Two Different Makeups

The husband needs to understand that a woman is different from a man. Her needs are different because she has a different makeup. The Bible teaches that.

You see, the woman brings in the feminine part — what we call the woman's touch — and she adds tenderness and love to the marital relationship. The man brings in masculinity and strength. He is ordained by God to be somebody the wife can admire and respect. She knows that when life gets tough she can count on her husband to seek God for the answers.

So, the man needs to learn about his wife, and the woman needs to understand her husband. They need to learn what God has said in His Word.

We find in Genesis, chapter 3, that Eve made a mistake by listening to the serpent and falling for his lies, but Adam just stood there and watched it happen. Then mankind found itself in a mess.

God had put extra responsibility on Adam to take the lead, and his wife was to mold and fashion herself after him. But Adam wimped out on her when he should have stood his ground against the serpent's lies. Paul, writing to Timothy, says the woman was deceived but the man was not. (1 Tim. 2:14.) Man was blatantly rebellious, and sin came upon the earth because of it.

So, What Is Marriage All About?

Let me remind you of what marriage is, and is not.

First of all, as we found out earlier, marriage is a covenant of companionship between a man and a woman — not a man and a man, or a woman and a woman. It was created, ordained and instituted by God and is governed by

God's law of love. Marriage is the foundation of the Church and of society.

So, why did God bring the woman to the man in the beginning?

Was it to help him fulfill his ministry? No. He was already fulfilling his calling before she was brought on the scene.

Was it to help him fulfill his walk with God and to be a better person? No. He was already fulfilled in his walk with God. He communed with God in the cool of the day. (Gen. 3:8.) So in the beginning man didn't have any sin in his life!

Then why did God bring the woman, the helper, to man in the first place? Because it was not good that man should be alone.

Marriage is not just for the propagation of the human race and for the replenishing of the earth. It is not just a way that man can fulfill his desire for sex. Neither is it just so a man and woman can raise kids or build a career together or work together in ministry.

Marriage is not to be changed, altered or governed by society, by man or by religious theologians.

Marriage was put into force by God as a way to rid a man and woman of their loneliness and to bring each of them a companion to share life's adventures with them.

Two people get married because they want to share life's experiences with each other. By joining themselves and becoming one, they have fellowship and companionship as they are working together through life. They have sweet communion with one another. That's what marriage is all about.

Adam said of the woman, "She is bone of my bones and flesh of my flesh. We will merge and become one. We will cleave together, join together, mold ourselves together." (Gen. 2:23,24.)

Marriage Is a Give-and-Take Proposition

What is marriage all about? It's about being able to communicate and share from your heart with your spouse. The world may be caving in around you, but you know that you can go home and pour out your heart to your mate. You can weep and cry and be yourself, without being ashamed. Nobody on planet Earth will love you the way your spouse will. There is only one being in all creation who loves you more than your spouse, and that is the Lord Jesus Christ.

In Ephesians, chapter 5, when Paul was writing to the church of Ephesus, he likened the relationship of the husband and wife to the Christian and the Lord. As believers, we are married unto the Lord and have become one spirit with Him; so also do the husband and wife become one spirit with each other.

The husband is to love his wife, to oversee and protect her, and to provide and care for her. The wife is to mold herself to her husband, to adapt herself to him and to care for him.

Marriage is a process of give and take until God just takes those two people by His hand and by His Word and molds them together. They become one, and they have communion with one another.

It's a shame that a wife doesn't feel she can go to her husband to pour out her heart and share her hurts. Instead, she has to go to another woman or to a pastor or even to a psychiatrist.

She should be able to go to her husband with a problem and not be ridiculed or put down or made a spectacle of. She should be able to open herself to him, allowing her innermost feelings to be exposed, and not feel ashamed. She should expect love and concern and care to be extended from him to her.

The husband should feel just as comfortable about going to his wife with his problems. He may appear to be Mr. Macho, the man who can do whatever is needed in life; but there are times when his heart is breaking. When he has gone through a mess in life, he must know that he can expose those hurts to his wife without being thought of as a wimp.

You see, the husband-and-wife relationship has to be this way.

Now in God's eyes, the number-one rule for marriage is that a believer should not marry an unbeliever. Why? Because as we find in Second Corinthians 6:14, light and darkness do not work together. The believer and the unbeliever will have trouble. There is no communion between them. Let's look at a situation that occurred with the prophet Elijah.

Elijah's Pity Party

In First Kings, chapter 19, we find Elijah crying out to God, "I wish I were dead!" But he didn't really want to be dead. Queen Jezebel had already threatened that she would kill him the next day. Had he really wanted to die, he could have just stayed there in town. But, instead, he ran out into the wilderness, sat down under a juniper tree and was having a pity party.

Now this was the same prophet who had called fire down from heaven, killed all the false prophets and outrun the king's horses and chariots. I mean, Elijah was a super-duper macho man. But now this Mr. Macho was just sitting there under the juniper tree and crying out to God.

Elijah poured out his heart, exposing his insecurities and frustrations, and God heard all of it. He listened to all of Elijah's crying and fussing and carrying on. Finally, God said to him, "What are you doing here?" Then He told Elijah to get up and go. You see, God didn't give up on Elijah; He just kept on loving him. God took care of him while he was down; then He raised him up and sent him on his way.

That could be a picture of the husband-and-wife relationship.

When the husband gets so frustrated that, like Elijah, he just crawls under a tree, the wife should crawl under there with him and just let him get all those feelings out of his system.

Now notice God just let Elijah blow off all the steam that had built up within him. When the husband wants to blow off and fuss and carry on, one of the worst things the wife could say is: "Now, honey, you can do it." He doesn't want to hear her say that. He just wants her to be quiet and let him have a pity party for a while.

You see, God didn't tell Elijah that he could do anything until he had finished with his pity party. Then God stirred him until he was up and moving again.

This can happen the same way with the wife. When she comes home after a bad day, with all those feelings of insecurity, she just wants to rest on her husband's shoulder for a little while and let him give her a hug. But instead of being a comfort to her, he says, "What's the matter with you? You know what the Word says!"

So, you see, marriage is a commitment between a man and woman to be each other's best friend. Nobody on planet Earth should love them more than their spouse.

That's just the way it should be, because that's the way God intended it to be. But when it isn't that way, the husband and wife will have trouble. That's why God said the husband must leave father and mother. A mom and dad can't love their son the way a wife loves her husband. Marital love supersedes Mom and Dad's love.

In marital love, the husband and the wife are to give themselves totally to one another. He gives himself totally to her; she gives herself totally to him. They become one together as they begin their walk in that covenant of companionship, that communion.

That's what God intended. That's what marriage is.

Abide by God's Rules for Marriage

In Mark, chapter 12, we find the Sadducees asking Jesus about a woman who had been married to each of seven brothers before they died. They said to Him:

> In the resurrection therefore, when
> they shall rise, whose wife shall she be of
> them? for the seven had her to wife (v. 23).

Jesus answered:

> Do ye not therefore err, because ye
> know not the scriptures, neither the power
> of God? (v. 24).

The Lord was saying to them that when you don't know the Scriptures and you don't know the power of God, you will find yourself in error. Then He said:

> For when they shall rise from the dead,
> they neither marry, nor are given in mar-
> riage (v. 25).

What does this mean? That marriage in heaven will not be a part of life the way it is here on earth. But as long as we are here, marriage will still be in operation; society can't get rid of it, and we can't change its rules. We have to do just as Jesus said.

We can't bend to the liberal theologians of today who want to put their rules and their laws into operation. Just because something isn't convenient to their doctrine, they want to change their beliefs. We can't do that.

We have to abide by the Word of God. God says it is still His fashion for the husband to take the lead and for his wife to follow him. The two of them are to be walking together as heirs of the grace of this life, praying together, raising up a family together, fighting off the obstacles of life together. After facing difficulties and tests and trials, they will be walking the way God called them to walk. That is God's will.

Now, who should, and should not, be married?

That's a really good question. Let's find some answers.

CHAPTER 4

Who Should Be Married?

Let's look again in Matthew, chapter 19, where the Pharisees had asked Jesus about divorce. We will get into the subject of divorce later. But I want to consider another aspect of marriage by asking this question: Who should, or should not, be married?

First, Who Should Not Be Married?

Jesus, in talking with the Pharisees about why divorce would be allowed, described adultery as the only acceptable reason for divorce. He said to them:

> **Whosoever shall put away his wife,**
> **except it be for fornication, and shall**

**marry another, committeth adultery: and
whoso marrieth her which is put away doth
commit adultery.**

Matthew 19:9

Then the disciples responded to His comment, saying:

**If the case of the man be so with his
wife, it is not good to marry.**

Matthew 19:10

In other words, if a man is divorced for any reason
other than sexual misconduct by his wife and then gets
remarried, he is seen as having committed adultery.

Under the Law, adultery was punishable by stoning. So,
the disciples were saying, "If there is even a chance of messing up, it would be better for him not to get married in the
first place."

Here was Jesus' response:

**But he said unto them, All men cannot
receive this saying, save they to whom it is
given.**

Matthew 19:11

What was Jesus saying here? He was telling them: "Don't throw the baby out with the bath water. Don't be afraid to make a mistake. Besides that, if you don't have the gift of being single, then it would be hard for you to stay single and still succeed in life."

You need to remember the norm in life: *It is not good to be alone.* That's what God had said in Genesis 2:18. What does it mean? That the single life is not the way God had planned for us to live.

Jesus was plainly telling us, "Not everybody can stay single."

The Single Life

In verse 12 Jesus describes to the disciples three types of eunuchs, or those who are capable of living a single life.

> **For there are some eunuchs, which were so born from their mother's womb....**
>
> **Matthew 19:12**

In other words, He was saying that some people are able to stay single from the time they are born. That's just the way they are.

**...and there are some eunuchs, which
were made eunuchs of men....**

Matthew 19:12

You need to understand how life was in those days. When a conquering army would capture an entire nation, they would take the young men in that country, separate them from their people and force them to stay single and celibate.

**...and there be eunuchs, which have
made themselves eunuchs for the kingdom
of heaven's sake. He that is able to receive
it, let him receive it.**

Matthew 19:12

Jesus was saying that not everybody is able to be like this, meaning it is the exception, not the norm.

What does this verse mean? That some people are born this way, while others were made to be this way through the conditions of life. But still others sell themselves out to God for the sake of God's kingdom and are able to overcome any sexual desires or other problems they may have. They can be totally fulfilled in their walk with the Lord.

If you intend to stay single, let it be for the right reasons. Don't do it because you once had a bad relationship in love and your feelings have been hurt, or because you are mad at somebody. Don't do it because some disaster happened in your life and you haven't let God heal you of it.

You see, there are people today who are staying single for all the wrong reasons — because of hurts or pressure, because of problems in their flesh or in their mind — and they are out of the will of God. They say, "My heart has been hurt so badly; I just can't trust anybody." That's selfishness and evidence that the person's past needs to be healed, letting go of **the former things** (Isa. 43:18).

God said that He would heal the brokenhearted. (Luke 4:18; Isa. 61:1.) That's why Jesus came.

If you are going to be single, do it for the kingdom of God's sake. Do it as unto the Lord. Do it because God has spoken to your heart that this is the lifestyle you are to live.

But, remember, this is the exception. Unless God speaks to your heart that you are to stay single, it would be wrong for you to do so.

⁂ ⁂ ⁂

 ## Then, Who Should Be Married?

I want you to see what the Word of God has to say. The apostle Paul is writing to the church at Corinth:

> **Now concerning the things whereof ye wrote unto me: It is good for a man not to touch a woman.**
>
> **1 Corinthians 7:1**

Now the phrase *to touch a woman* doesn't just mean to reach out physically and hold her hand. It means to touch her in lust or inflame her with passion.

In other words, this would be saying to a couple: "Don't go out parking and get each other all hot and bothered and so full of passion that you are ready to get off into sin."

> **Nevertheless, to avoid fornication** (sexual impurity, sexual immorality), **let every man have his own wife, and let every woman have her own husband.**
>
> **1 Corinthians 7:2**

Then in verse 7 Paul says:

> **For I would that all men were even as I
> myself. But every man hath his proper gift
> of God, one after this manner, and another
> after that.**

Paul was basically saying: "I have the gift to stay single, and I'm sold out to God. I have chosen this lifestyle and have done it for the kingdom of God. You would be better off if you could be like me, because I don't have these other problems."

Then he goes on talking about how the husband has to deal with his wife and how the wife has to deal with her husband.

But, you know, if you don't have the gift to stay single, you can't do it. That's why, as Paul says, every man has his proper gift. If you don't have the gift to stay complete and fulfilled and serving God as a single, you need to do what Paul says next:

> **I say therefore to the unmarried and
> widows, It is good for them if they abide
> even as I.**

But if they cannot contain, let them marry: for it is better to marry than to burn (with lust or passion).

1 Corinthians 7:8,9

You might ask, "But how do I know whether I'm supposed to get married?"

To the man, I would say this: If when approaching some gorgeous woman, you can just walk by her without getting all bothered and having to go and take a cold shower, you could probably stay single for the rest of your life.

To the woman, I would say: If when you see some good-looking guy, you don't start feeling kind of silly and thinking of wedding bells, you could probably stay single for the rest of your life.

But this is the thing: If you can't look and can't touch without having all those kinds of feelings and thoughts, then you need to be married.

As Paul was saying here, you ought to abide in your gift. If you are supposed to get married but don't, then you are in disobedience to God. If you are supposed to stay single, but instead you go out and start fooling around with the opposite sex, then you are in disobedience to God.

Now that doesn't mean you can start claiming some person as your mate because that's the one you want, or that you can get married for all the wrong reasons.

You still have to realize that it was God Who brought Eve to Adam and it was God Who joined them together. This still has to be done God's way, and you have to let Him do it.

God was busy in fellowship with Adam, and Adam was busy doing God's work. They were working and flowing together. Then one day Adam woke up after a deep sleep, and there stood this beautiful creature, which he named Woman. Then she joined with him in the garden, and they were happy together.

You see, you are to live in God and to fulfill your life in God's timing, then let God bring it together as He chooses. If you are supposed to get married, then at some point you will say: "Lord, I'm not happy and fulfilled being single; I'm ready for marriage."

Here's another point to consider: Christian men and women have absolutely no business fooling around sexually with each other, regardless of whether they plan to be married. They shouldn't be inflaming another person's sexual appetite. No wonder these people have trouble living for God.

Seek God First

Let's look again at the example of God's dealings with Adam and Eve.

God had laid out spiritual law which they were to follow at the time. Adam did not know another woman until she was formed for him by God. He had been busy serving the Lord, doing what God told him to do and securing his walk with God by fellowshipping with Him. He had been living by faith before God; then God saw his need and met it.

If you are a single person who wants God to bring the right person into your life, I will tell you how it can take place. The man has to get turned on to God and start doing everything God is calling him to do in his life, while the woman gets turned on to God and starts doing what God has called her to do in her life. Then God will work at bringing the two of you together.

But if the man is hitting every bar in town, thinking that if he finds a woman to marry, he will get saved, he is making a big mistake. It doesn't work that way.

You don't marry someone in order to become a Christian. You become a Christian first; then you will be able to find the person God intends for you to marry. You have to go where Christians are and get involved.

Single people who want to be married ought to first find out God's will for their lives. They need to make sure their lives are free of all the hurts, anxieties, frustrations and feelings of bad relationships from the past.

They have to get turned on to God and be serving Him from their hearts. As they are doing that, then God will cause another person who is serving Him to come across their path. Then the two of them will be equally yoked together.

But if some guy who is an emotional basket case was praying for God to send a woman into his life to be a blessing to him as his wife, God would be doing that woman an injustice to bring her on the scene. That guy is wanting the perfect woman in his life, and she would be slighted if she were to join herself with him. He is a real mess, and he needs to change first before taking on the responsibilities of marriage.

On the other hand, there might be a woman in church who is emotionally fragile. Because she has been hurt in life, she can break down in tears at the least little thing. She hasn't taken enough time to get herself healed up and secure in the Lord. Yet in spite of that, she is praying for God to send her Mr. Everything. She needs to allow time for the healing process to take place within her; then she can be the same kind of person she wants God to send to her. God wants the two of them to be equally yoked together.

Whether or not to marry is a question that should be seriously considered by every believer who is single. If that's your situation, remember to seek God first in your life. Don't put the desire for marriage above your desire for God. Give Him first place in your life; then He will be able to bring the right partner across your path in His timing.

CHAPTER 5

God's Number-One Rule Over Marriage

What is the number-one rule that governs marriage? It is a phrase found at the end of First Corinthians, chapter 7, verse 39:

> **The wife is bound by the law as long as her husband liveth; but if her husband be dead, she is at liberty to be married to whom she will; only in the Lord.**

God says that the number-one rule governing marriage is that believers are to marry *only in the Lord*. That means whatever else may happen in our lives, we first have to be right with God.

Notice it says the widow **is at liberty to be married to whom she will;** in other words, to anybody she wants, whether rich or poor, tall or short, handsome or ugly. That doesn't matter — as long as the man she marries is a believer.

You Become One With Your Spouse

Now look in First Corinthians, chapter 6:

> **Know ye not that your bodies are the members of Christ? shall I then take the members of Christ, and make them members of an harlot? God forbid.**
>
> **What? know ye not that he which is joined to an harlot is one body? for two, saith he, shall be one flesh.**
>
> **But he that is joined unto the Lord is one spirit.**
>
> **1 Corinthians 6:15-17**

This is saying that whenever a believer is married, he or she becomes one with their spouse.

But, Pastor, I'm married to a sinner.

Then you are one with that sinner.

This Scripture is saying: "Shall you as a member of the Body of Christ join yourself to a harlot? If you do, you become one with that person."

But I don't believe a sinner and a Christian can really be joined together.

Then you don't believe the Bible. Paul has said that when you are joined in marriage to another person, you become one with that person. That's why he says we are to be married **only in the Lord.**

Be Not Unequally Yoked With an Unbeliever

Now let's look at Second Corinthians, chapter 6. Again, Paul is speaking to the Body of Christ. In verse 14 he begins:

> **Be ye not unequally yoked together with unbelievers....**

Paul is saying that when a believer, who is joined with the Lord, yokes himself or herself with an unbeliever, who is joined with the devil, then there won't be any agreement there. The two of them will have problems.

So the number-one rule that God lays down about marriage is this: The believer must make sure he or she is marrying another believer.

No matter who you marry, whether believer or unbeliever, you will become one with that person.

Now, continuing in verse 14, we find the problem:

> ...for what fellowship hath righteousness with unrighteousness? and what communion hath light with darkness?

What agreement is there between the two?

None.

Why did God create marriage?

So that a man and woman could have companionship and sweet communion with one another.

A husband and wife should be able to open themselves up to their spouse and share their innermost secrets with one another. That's the kind of companionship and communion they should have together.

But God is saying that there will be real problems in the marriage of a believer and an unbeliever. There will be no companionship and communion between them. They will be defeating the whole purpose of marriage.

That's why parents need to teach their kids what marriage is all about. Their young daughters should be taught what to look for in a man and how to conduct themselves. Their young men should be taught how to treat a lady and how to conduct themselves around a young girl.

Young people today need to know what they should be looking for in marriage and why they need it in their lives. She shouldn't be marrying him just because he looks neat driving a sports car, and he shouldn't be marrying her just because she looks great wearing a miniskirt. It takes more than that to form a relationship. They need to find out what God says. There must be communion and companionship between them. That's what marriage is all about.

Paul goes on:

> **And what concord hath Christ with Belial? or what part hath he that believeth with an infidel?**
>
> **And what agreement hath the temple of God with idols?**
>
> **2 Corinthians 6:15,16**

You see, there is no agreement, no communion, no fellowship, no companionship between a believer and an unbeliever. So God's number-one rule for the believer is simple: Don't marry an unbeliever!

What To Do If Already Married to an Unbeliever

Now somebody might say, "But you're too late; I'm already married to an unbeliever. So what do I do?"

If you are married to an unbeliever, you probably realize that everything I'm telling you is the absolute truth. You are looking for the strength, the companionship, the compassion, the communion with your spouse; but it just isn't there.

You have to do according to the Word of God. The only recourse is found in First Peter, chapter 3.

> **Likewise, ye wives, be in subjection to your own husbands; that, if any obey not the word, they also may without the word** (or preaching) **be won by the conversation** (or conduct) **of the wives;**

While they behold your chaste conver-sation (or manner of life) **coupled with fear.**

Whose adorning let it not be that out-ward adorning of plaiting the hair, and of wearing of gold, or of putting on of apparel;

But let it be the hidden man of the heart, in that which is not corruptible, even the ornament of a meek and quiet spirit, which is in the sight of God of great price.

1 Peter 3:1-4

If you are a woman whose husband is an unbeliever, you need to realize that you can't win him over by preaching at him all the time and hounding him about becoming a Christian. Neither can you win him by compromising your walk with Christ and trying to be like him. Jesus Christ is your spiritual head, not that man.

Now, for there to be order in your home, the apostle Peter says, you are to submit to your husband domestically. The husband is still head of the house. You are to obey him and honor him as head of your home, regardless of whether or not he is fulfilling his job as husband. Then God will be able to work in your situation.

You have to live the life of Jesus Christ in front of your husband and walk in love even when he doesn't. You have to be a Christian when he is acting like a heathen. You should take care of yourself and look good, but that's just on the outside; it takes some work on the inside to get the job done.

So whether it's the husband or the wife who is lost, as the believing spouse you have to do what the Word says through Peter. And you have to keep working at it.

You have to be a greater influence for Christ in your home than your spouse is for the devil. Light will win out over darkness — not by words, but by actions and deeds, by living the kind of life Jesus lived here on earth.

You have to be so salty that you get your spouse thirsty for Jesus Christ. You have to do your part by loving and praying and caring for your spouse, regardless of whether you can see any results on the outside.

Only by planting that seed, God says, will you have an

opportunity to bring your spouse into the kingdom of God. Just know that it will work. God's Word won't return void. (Isa. 55:11.) Praise God.

God's Law of Love

So, what is the law of God that governs marriage? The same law that governs the Church: the royal law of love that's found in James 2:8. Without God's love, a marriage will never make it.

In Romans 13:8 the apostle Paul says:

> **Owe no man any thing, but to love one another: for he that loveth another hath fulfilled the law.**

A husband and a wife owe it to each other to love one another.

Paul continues in verses 9 and 10 to describe God's law of love:

> **For this, Thou shalt not commit adultery, Thou shalt not kill, Thou shalt not steal, Thou shalt not bear false witness, Thou shalt not covet; and if there be any**

**other commandment, it is briefly compre-
hended in this saying, namely, Thou shalt
love thy neighbour as thyself.**

**Love worketh no ill to his neighbour:
therefore love is the fulfilling of the law.**

This Scripture is saying that if we love each other we
won't be hurting one another.

As was stated earlier, marriage is a covenant of companionship, ordained by God, bringing a man and woman
together to make them one. The law of love governs their
relationship.

That love won't cause people to commit adultery, or to
steal, or to take advantage of other people. Love will cause
them to open themselves to others by exposing both their
faults and their strengths. They will care for others and
pray with others and be sensitive to one another's needs.
That love will lead them to be a companion and to produce
sweet communion with their spouse.

I want you to realize this fact: There has never been a
Christian couple to end up in divorce when they have really
been practicing the law of love.

Now I didn't say Christians have never been in the divorce court. Unfortunately, many have. But the difference has been when both husband and wife are Christians who have allowed the law of love to work in their lives.

Love works no ill; therefore, love overcomes all things. First Peter 4:8 says:

> **And above all things have fervent love for one another, for "love will cover a multitude of sins"** (NKJV).

If all Christians would be walking in love, they wouldn't find themselves in a bad situation with their spouse. Love will forgive. Love will overlook. Love will cover.

Learn To Practice Love

The reason Christians fail is because they haven't learned to practice the law of love. According to Galatians 5:22, love is a fruit of the Spirit. That means it can grow.

You might ask, "How do I make it grow?"

It grows by acting on the Word of God. (1 John 2:5.)

God's love is not governed by feelings, emotions or situations. It's governed by the Word. What does that mean?

When strife comes in, love seeks for a reconciliation and recovery. When there is division, love reaches out and brings harmony.

Love is quick to forgive, quick to repent, quick to overlook problems.

Love puts a bad situation behind and doesn't dig it back up again.

Love doesn't wait on feelings to come before saying, "I love you."

Love in one spouse says to the other: "I'm one with you and you're one with me, so no devil in hell is going to put asunder what God has put together. We're going to stand this test. I'm going to say, `I love you,' until I really feel it."

But I want you to know something: husband and wife are two parts of one. Marriage is like a coin. It takes both the head and the tail to make it work. It takes the husband and wife working together for success.

A husband can't be saying to his wife, "I love you," while his wife says to him, "I can't stand you."

The wife can't be saying to her husband, "I love you," while he says, "I'm going to take advantage of you."

To succeed, it takes both of them operating in the law of love together.

That means they both have to put their feelings aside. They have to look at one another and accept them exactly as they are. They each have to say to the other:

"Whether or not you ever change, I love you just the way you are. I'm one with you, and you're one with me. We are exposing ourselves to one another. You can see my strengths and weaknesses; I can see yours. But we're going to love each other in spite of that.

"When you are weak, I'm going to try to help you and strengthen you, not in a condemning way but in a good way. When I'm weak, I believe you will stand with me, strengthening me and helping me. Where we each are strong, we will complement one another."

If the husband and wife will learn to walk in love, then they can walk in victory.

God set down the institution of marriage between the husband and the wife so that He could work His will in them. Their lives will be fulfilled as they are caring for one another under God's law of love.

But what if one or both of the marriage partners are not willing to live under God's law of love? What if they go against the marriage covenant they had entered at the beginning? Let's consider this aspect by looking further into God's Word.

CHAPTER 6

When the Marriage Covenant Is Broken

I want us to look in chapter 2 of the book of Malachi. You might ask, "What would Malachi be teaching besides tithing?" You would be amazed!

You see, Malachi worked to get God's people straightened out before he taught them on tithing. He probably figured that if they weren't living for God, they wouldn't tithe anyway.

God, in speaking through the prophet Malachi, was talking about Judah. Let's read the whole passage of Scripture first, then break it down verse by verse.

Judah hath dealt treacherously, and an abomination is committed in Israel and in

Jerusalem; for Judah hath profaned the holiness of the Lord which he loved, and hath married the daughter of a strange god.

The Lord will cut off the man that doeth this, the master and the scholar, out of the tabernacles of Jacob, and him that offereth an offering unto the Lord of hosts.

And this have ye done again, covering the altar of the Lord with tears, with weeping, and with crying out, insomuch that he regardeth not the offering any more, or receiveth it with good will at your hand.

Yet ye say, Wherefore? Because the Lord hath been witness between thee and the wife of thy youth, against whom thou hast dealt treacherously: yet is she thy companion, and the wife of thy covenant.

And did not he make one? Yet had he the residue of the spirit. And wherefore

one? That he might seek a godly seed.
Therefore take heed to your spirit, and let
none deal treacherously against the wife of
his youth.

Malachi 2:11-15

A Believer Married to an Unbeliever

Judah hath dealt treacherously, and an
abomination is committed in Israel and in
Jerusalem....

Malachi 2:11

Now the word *treacherously* in the Hebrew means
"unfaithfully."[1] In other words, Judah had been unfaithful,
and an abomination had been committed in Israel. Then
God called what is mentioned in the rest of this verse an
abomination. It says:

...for Judah hath profaned the holiness
of the Lord which he loved... (v. 11).

So, what did Judah do to get God so upset? It tells us
further in verse 11:

...and hath married the daughter of a strange god.

God was upset because one of His precious children had married a sinner, which ruined everything God had set up for them. That isn't God's will. It isn't what God wants. God says, "That's wrong!"

Now look at verse 12:

> **The Lord will cut off the man that doeth this, the master and the scholar, out of the tabernacles of Jacob, and him that offereth an offering unto the Lord of hosts.**

In other words, God was saying: "Because you have done this, you won't prosper now but will have troubles and struggles. You have opened yourself up to be defeated."

Verse 13 says:

> **And this have ye done again, covering the altar of the Lord with tears, with weeping, and with crying out, insomuch that he regardeth not the offering any more, or receiveth it with good will at your hand.**

God is saying: "You have broken My number-one rule in marriage by becoming unequally yoked with an unbeliever. By walking in the flesh, you are causing all kinds of problems, and it's hard for Me to bless you."

This says God wouldn't receive their offerings and couldn't answer their prayers. Why?

The Marriage Covenant Was Broken

Verse 14 tells us:

> **Yet ye say, Wherefore? Because the Lord hath been witness between thee and the wife of thy youth, against whom thou hast dealt treacherously** (or unfaithfully): **yet is she thy companion, and the wife of thy covenant.**

God is saying: "You were married to the wife of your youth. She was your companion, and you entered into covenant together. But now, because you have cast her off and have gone after a strange woman, you have profaned what I told you to do. You have broken the marriage covenant that you had made with the right one so that you could go out after the wrong one."

Not only do we find teaching on marriage here, but now we begin to find some teaching on divorce.

Notice what God is saying: If a husband begins to deal unfaithfully and do wrong toward his wife, he is inviting trouble into his life. His prayers will be hindered, his offerings won't be received and he won't prosper in life.

This ties in with First Peter 3:7. What did Peter say? That husbands are to dwell with their wives according to knowledge, giving honor to them, treating them as the weaker vessel and being heirs together of the grace of this life. Why? So that their prayers would not be hindered.

If a husband and wife don't keep the right relationship in their covenant of marriage, then hindrances will come as the result. Their walk with God will be blocked. Their prayer life will be hindered. The success and prosperity of their lives together will be prevented. In effect, God's perfect will and plan for their lives will be halted.

It's Important To Allow Some Time for Engagement

When a couple comes to me and says they are ready to get married, I always say to them: "I want you to be engaged for six months." Many times this will sound too strong, and they will say, "That's too long a time. We're in love!"

But if they really are in love, they will still be in love six months later. In my opinion, six months should be a minimum time of engagement.

But why make a couple wait six months?

Because I know the consequences of their making the wrong choice and marrying out of the will of God. If they don't get married in the right way and to the right person, they will be hindering their spiritual walk with God.

I expect a man and woman to take some time and get to know each other. If he is going to dwell with her according to knowledge, as First Peter 3:7 says, then he really should have some knowledge before he starts dwelling with her. They each should better understand the person they will be living with for the rest of their lives.

God says that what people do and the decisions they make in their marriage will affect every area of their lives.

ॐ ॐ ॐ

 ## The Marriage Covenant Is Made By Vows

Now let's read on in Malachi, chapter 2, looking again at what it says in verse 14:

> **...the Lord hath been witness between thee and the wife of thy youth...and the wife of thy covenant.**

Now as I have pointed out several times in this study, marriage is a covenant. It's the joining together, the coming together, of a husband and wife. God witnesses that covenant, and it is established by their vows — not by sexual intercourse.

A man and woman become husband and wife when they *say* their vows to one another, then they are pronounced husband and wife. So, this covenant of marriage is formed by words, not necessarily by actions.

How do we know that? Galatians, chapter 3, verse 6 says, **Abraham believed God, and it was accounted to him for righteousness.** The outward act of covenant, or circumcision, was a confirmation of the covenant that had already been established in the spirit. (Rom. 4:11.) So a covenant is a spiritual agreement between two people before the physical act is performed by them.

That's why God's number-one rule over marriage must be observed: He says we are not to be unequally yoked – a believer with an unbeliever.

Again, the marriage covenant is a spiritual covenant. As God says, **...what communion hath light with darkness?** (2 Cor. 6:14). In other words, it's hard for the two parties to have spiritual agreement if they don't come together. That's why they get married: for communion, for companionship. It is for them to draw together and to share life's experiences.

Marriage is the second strongest covenant known by man. The first strongest covenant is our relationship with Jesus Christ. So, the marriage covenant is likened unto the relationship we have with Jesus Christ.

God Witnesses the Marriage

Notice here that God witnesses the formation of this covenant of marriage. In other words, God goes to weddings. It says this right here in Malachi 2, verse 14:

...the Lord hath been witness between thee and the wife of thy youth...and the wife of thy covenant.

So, when do a man and woman become husband and wife? This seems to be a sticky question.

Usually, people will say, "Well, the marriage isn't consummated yet; they haven't been on their honeymoon." Most think that it takes the sexual relationship to consummate the wedding ceremony. But it does not. Their sexual relationship is merely a privilege that they have after marriage.

Then when are a man and woman married?

The moment they are pronounced husband and wife by the preacher.

But they haven't had sexual relations yet.

Well, that isn't the preacher's fault! It will come in time. Now that they are married, they have that privilege. But just because they haven't had sex yet doesn't mean they aren't married. Suppose a man went out and had sex with five or six women. Does that mean he would be married to all of them? No! Sex isn't what makes a marriage.

Marriage is the result of the covenant a man and woman entered when they made their vows of commitment to one another.

Think for a moment about what got you saved. Romans 10:9,10 says if you believe in your heart that Jesus died for you and that God raised Him from the dead, you will be saved. It says with the heart you believe unto righteousness and with the mouth confession is made unto salvation. So, when does salvation come to you? When you have confessed your commitment to Christ Jesus as your Lord. You enter into covenant with God through a commitment made with vows spoken out of your mouth.

A man and woman enter into covenant as husband and wife the moment they speak forth words in the marriage ceremony like, "I give myself to you." They have pledged themselves to one another when they say, "I do." Then God witnesses the formation of that covenant between them.

Wedding Is More Than Just a Ceremony

It's important, then, for a man and woman to investigate beforehand what they will be pledging to one another in their marriage vows.

When I will be performing a wedding, I take special time with the couple, because I want them to understand the commitment they will be making to one another. I take them through the wedding ceremony and explain their vows to them.

Now my wedding ceremony usually lasts about forty-five minutes. I take them through several Scriptures on marriage. After asking if they are saved, I have them make a profession of their vows to one another. Then we have communion, and I pray the blessings of God over them.

Why put such emphasis on a marriage ceremony? Because God puts emphasis on it. He witnesses what two people say to each other when they are forming their covenant together as husband and wife. Then He holds them accountable for the vows they have made to one another.

In Malachi, chapter 2, we see God getting aggravated at Judah for going against the marriage vows he had spoken to his wife and for pulling away from her. God says to him: "Because you are not honoring your commitment, I can't bless you. I can't hear your prayers, and your offerings aren't worth anything. You have created a mess for your life by not doing what you said you would do. You aren't fulfilling the covenant you had made to your wife."

Now why does God want His people to know what they are doing when forming a marriage covenant? Look at verse 15:

> **And did not he make one? Yet had he**
> **the residue of the spirit....**

You see, God made a man to be one with his wife.

But what is meant by the phrase *residue of the spirit?* The residue is that which is left after everything else has been rinsed out. When you rinse out a jar, the only thing left is the residue. Everything that could be flushed out has been.

What is God saying here? That He wants a husband and wife to come together to the point that they are one and that the only thing left in them is God.

He wants to wash out of them everything that would hinder their walk as husband and wife — all the selfishness and sin, all the worldliness and the carnality. He doesn't want them looking around to see if they can find somebody better. He wants to wash out of them everything that would keep them from being one together.

He wants to clean out a husband and wife until He has all the residue of their spirits. In other words, until He has nothing there but a pure marriage of two people joined together in like mind, in singleness of purpose, in one vision, in one accord.

God's Reason for a Good, Strong Marriage

Now why does God want the husband and wife to be that strong? Let's read on in verse 15. He says:

...And wherefore one? (or, Why does God push you to become one?) **That he might seek a godly seed....**

The reason God wants a good marriage between a godly husband and a godly wife is so that He can produce not only blessings in their lives but a godly seed as well. In other words, godly children will be produced by them, and they will be blessed; then God will be able to work through that next generation.

The more Mom and Dad are walking together as one, serving God and doing what God has called them to do, the more apt their children will be to follow Him and do what He wants them to do.

God is saying that not only will marriage affect the husband and wife, but how they treat one another as husband and wife will affect their children.

God's Warning About Marriage

Now let's read on in verse 15 and see what else God says. Here He is giving a warning:

...Therefore take heed to your spirit....

In other words, God is saying that marriage is a spiritual relationship between a man and a woman. Do you see that? It begins in the spirits of these two people, then works its way until it is manifested in their flesh, and God has His way in their lives.

Again, I want to point out that marriage is not a physical act between husband and wife, but a spiritual commitment they have made to one another. The man and woman become husband and wife by first entering into a spiritual relationship. Then they begin to develop the mental relationship and have the privilege of enjoying the physical relationship as a result of their commitment to one another.

God is saying, "You need to take heed to your spirit." Verse 15 ends:

...and let none deal treacherously (or unfaithfully) **against the wife of his youth.**

Now we have seen what marriage is: a covenant of companionship between two, or a covenanting together that makes them one.

So, God is serious about marriage. He wants a man and woman to have a holy family, a holy seed. He wants them to be blessed and to prosper. He wants their prayers to work. He wants them to flow together as one, so that they will be powerful and anointed. Then nothing will be impossible unto them. Praise God!

But as we have seen, problems do arise within a marriage to cause a breaking up of the vows that were made in the beginning between the husband and the wife. The result, then, is divorce. So let's look at the subject of divorce.

CHAPTER 7

What Is Divorce?

Let's examine further the words God speaks through the prophet Malachi:

> **For the Lord, the God of Israel, saith that *he hateth putting away*: for one covereth violence with his garment, saith the Lord of hosts: therefore take heed to your spirit, that ye deal not treacherously.**
>
> **Malachi 2:16**

Notice this verse of Scripture says God *hateth putting away*. The phrase *putting away* here means divorce. So, this is clearly saying that God hates divorce. But He doesn't hate the divorced person.

What is divorce? I will give you a definition. Divorce is

the dissolving of the marriage covenant between a husband and a wife, the breaking up of their covenant of companionship. But it is also the breaking of God's law of love.

As we mentioned earlier, God's number-one rule governing marriage is that a believer should not marry an unbeliever, and God's number-one law is the law of love.

In John 13:34 Jesus said, **A new commandment I give unto you, That ye love one another; as I have loved you, that ye also love one another.** As believers, we are to love one another as He loved us.

That's the law that governs the Church. In James 2:8 it is called **the royal law.** Romans 13:10 says, **Love worketh no ill to his neighbour.** Love would never commit adultery. It would never do anything to hurt another person.

As God is telling us in Malachi 2:16, if the husband were walking in the law of love, he would hate divorce and would not be dealing treacherously with his wife.

Divorce Starts in the Heart

Now let me point out something else God had said in Malachi 2:16:

...therefore take heed to your spirit,

that ye deal not treacherously.

What does He mean by saying *take heed to your spirit?*

Divorce starts in the heart; it does not start in the bed-room of a strange woman.

Divorce does not take place in a courtroom; it takes place first in the heart of the husband or the wife.

Now the divorce might be manifested and be finalized in the courtroom, but it really happened long before the husband and wife ever stood before the judge. It happened long before either of them ever got involved with another woman or another man, or actually broke away from their spouse. It started first in their heart.

Somewhere along the way, there had to be a breakdown between the spouse and his (or her) commitment to God. That person acted against the law of love and went contrary to everything God has said in His Word.

Then that breakdown with God caused a breakdown in their marriage, which ended with a dissolving of the covenant they had formed together in the beginning.

God hates that!

Unfortunately, divorce is sometimes necessary. God says there are times when it must take place. Divorce was put in as the remedy for serious marital problems. But it was never intended as the easy way out. It is not a cure-all; nor is it just a way to help people be free as a bird so that they never have another problem.

Why God Hates Divorce

Why does God hate divorce? There are basically three reasons.

First, God hates divorce because it will hinder people's spiritual walk.

I will use the husband as an example of one who is facing divorce. His spirit is wounded, and his relationship with God is changed. His prayers are hindered as he struggles in his walk with Christ. That's what Malachi was describing in verses 12 and 13 of chapter 2.

Secondly, God hates divorce because it hurts both the husband and the wife. In the beginning he supposedly loved and committed himself to her, and she made a commitment to him; but then problems arose, with divorce being the result. Neither of them will come out unscathed afterward. They both will be scarred because of it.

Then the divorce will affect not only the husband and wife but their two families as well. It will also have an effect on any love relationship that may develop with another individual. Then those two people will face another kind of struggle; they will have problems, and it won't be easy for them.

The third reason God hates divorce is because of the effect it will have on the children of that marriage. Hurt and pain will be brought into their lives, and they will have to be healed of it.

The Effect of Divorce
Can Last for Years

I have never been divorced, and Bonnie and I have been married for over twenty years. But I have known the result of divorce because I came from a divorced home.

Divorce had an impact on the first twenty years of my life, and still affects me in some ways to this day. I have tried to let it have a positive influence on the way I deal with my wife and children; but it has played a major role in my life and has affected my mother as well.

My mom was divorced when I was two years old and was remarried two years later, so my stepfather is the only dad I have ever known. To show you how divorce can have an impact on people many years later, I will share an incident that occurred when I was about twelve years old.

We had gotten a little plot of land and built a home. Then my dad, who was sort of a fix-it man, decided to put in a furnace that would heat the whole house. Though I was only a boy of twelve, I was right there helping him.

It was in the fall, so it was already getting cold outside, and it was wet and muddy as well. We had to crawl under the house to put in all the pipes, but we got it done, and it worked.

Now it had been ten years since my mom had been divorced and eight years since she had remarried. She and I were always close because we had been through so much together, and I was her oldest child. She treated me with respect and love, and as more of an adult than a child; so I was fairly mature for my age, even at twelve. I don't remember much of a childhood because I was always having to jump in there and help to get things done.

When I came home from school one day, I noticed that something was wrong with Mom. I could tell that she was upset. I said, "What is it, Mom? What's the matter?"

"Oh, nothing," she said.

"Now, what's wrong, Mom?"

"Well, I noticed that your dad isn't wearing his wedding ring. He hasn't had it on for three or four days now." At that time my dad worked as a truck driver, and he would be gone away from home a couple of days at a time.

Then Mom said: "He says that the ring was a little big on his finger and that he might have lost it in the mud when you two were fixing the furnace underneath the house. But I don't know. When you've been done wrong once, it's hard not to feel like it might happen to you again. He could have left that ring in a hotel room when he was with some floozy."

Now my dad loved my mom, and he would never do anything to hurt her. He was a good, moral man. Though he wasn't a Christian, he loved me with a love that most

Christians never showed. He didn't cuss; he didn't smoke; he didn't run around. He worked hard and taught me how to work. He put some good work ethics in me, taught me a lot about morality and made sure his kids were in church.

My dad had never given my mom any reason to doubt his love and faithfulness to her, but she was reacting out of hurt from the past. It wasn't what he had done but what she remembered from ten years before. She was still going through pain, resentment, doubt and fear because of what had already been done to her.

Even though I was only twelve, I could still see that, and I was really concerned about it. I knew what my mom had been through before, and I didn't want it to happen again. But I loved that man; he was the only dad I had ever known. So, I went outside and walked around for a while; then I prayed, "God, please don't let this happen. If there is anything I can do to help, show me."

Then I heard the Lord speaking to my heart and saying, "Get your light and go look under the house." So I got a flashlight and crawled under there, retracing my steps. I said, "Lord, I just know it's here; show me where it is."

With the flashlight in my hand, I crawled about ten or fifteen feet on that muddy, wet ground when something like a glittery light caught my eye. I crawled over to it, and there was my dad's little gold wedding band with just a small portion of it stuck out of the mud. I pulled it up and crawled out of there, just thanking God.

I hurried inside and said, "Mom, you don't have to doubt Dad anymore. It was under the house where he told you it was." Then she cried and I cried, and we prayed, and she was healed that evening. Thank God for a simple little prayer that was really a miraculous move of God.

Now here's my point: Though my mom was forced into a divorce, and though it was the only option she had at the time, it was still hurting her ten years later.

That's why God hates divorce.

He knows what it will do to a husband and a wife. He knows how it will alter their walk with Him and with each other and the effect it will have on their kids.

He also knows how divorced men and women will be treated by many churches. They will get thrown over and made to sit with the lepers, because they are seen as having committed the unpardonable sin and can never be used by God anymore. But that's wrong. We will deal further with this idea later.

We can see now that God hates divorce. Why? Because it affects a person's walk with God; it affects his walk with another person; and it affects the generation that comes after him.

Hardness of Heart

Now let's look again in Matthew, chapter 19. I want you to see something here. Divorce always starts in the heart, then manifests in the flesh, and it will always end up causing problems.

In verse 3 the Pharisees came and asked Jesus if they could get a divorce for just any reason. Then in verse 7 they asked Him why Moses allowed divorce.

The Lord answered them in verse 8, giving the only reason for divorce:

> **He saith unto them, Moses because of the hardness of your hearts suffered you to put away your wives: but from the beginning it was not so.**

What was the cause of divorce? Hardness of heart.

What did Malachi say to do? Take heed to your spirit, or your heart.

So, where does divorce begin? In your heart.

Why does divorce happen? Because of the hardness of one or both hearts of those involved.

Why is there divorce?

Because either the husband or the wife, maybe both, hardened their heart against the law of love. They chose to go against God's Word. They decided to do their own thing instead of fulfilling their vows which God had called them to do.

Divorce, then, is the dissolving of marriage, and it is caused because of sin and the hardness of the heart.

Divorce is the result of one or both parties hardening their hearts and refusing to allow God's law of love to rule over them.

I don't know of any couple involved in a divorce who hugged and kissed and congratulated each other, saying, "I'll miss you. How about lunch next week?" That just isn't how it works.

Sin, hardness of heart and selfishness are what rule divorce.

What is sin? A selfish decision to disobey God and hurt others.

What causes divorce? Sin and hardness of heart.

What is the result? It turns one or both of them into selfish people, instead of those who give to others. They don't care about their spouse. They only want their own desires fulfilled. Therefore, they will deal unfaithfully and treacherously with that person they are against.

That rules divorce, and God says He is against it.

Now we will be looking into the subject of divorce, both scripturally and unscripturally – what God says about divorce between believers and unbelievers. We won't be skirting any issue.

CHAPTER 8

Scriptural Divorce

First of all, let's deal with divorce between believers. What are the grounds that allow two believers to be divorced?

As we have already pointed out, all divorce is a result of sin but not all divorce is sinful.

Why?

Because God did not initiate or institute divorce; divorce was man's idea. It was a result of the hardness of their heart.

In Matthew, chapter 19, Jesus said Moses gave the people a law of divorcement. In other words, Moses came up with a law to regulate divorce. But divorce was already going on before he ever gave the people a writing of divorcement or laws they could follow. Therefore, man initiated divorce, and God gave Moses certain laws as a way to regulate it among His covenant children.

Jesus was saying: "Sin is what causes divorce. When you harden your heart to the law of God and turn away from Him, refusing to submit to His rules, the end result is a dividing, a dissolving and a tearing apart of the marriage covenant."

Moses went before God and said, "Lord, I need some help with this." So God began to regulate divorce by pointing out what was scriptural and unscriptural and what was acceptable and unacceptable.

God was saying: "I hate all of it, because it's going to hurt My people. They will have to recover and be restored and healed and helped. But I will regulate it by giving some guidelines for them to follow."

Religious Argument for Divorce

Now I want to look again in Matthew, chapter 19. Remember, the Lord Jesus Christ was asked by the Pharisees in verse 3:

Is it lawful for a man to put away his
wife for every cause?

He had answered them by saying: "No, God didn't create it that way. He created man and woman to be married, to become one flesh and to enjoy their lives together."

Anybody religious will always be trying to defend themselves. That's what the Pharisees did in verse 7:

They say unto him, Why did Moses
then command to give a writing of divorce-
ment, and to put her away?

You can always tell that you are in hot water when you start trying to defend your argument. After you have argued a point, and somebody comes back at you with what the Word of God says, if you continue arguing, you will be missing God.

The Pharisees weren't looking at God's Word and quoting Scripture. They had come up with their own religious idea of what they wanted to do. Religion is always pleasing to the flesh.

They were asking Jesus if they could be divorced for any cause. In other words, they were saying: "We want to have a greasy-grace religion with God so that we can keep living in our sin and get by with it. We don't want You coming along and rocking our boat." They kept coming at Jesus with an argument, but He kept giving them the Word.

When you find yourself making an argument against the Word of God, you had better repent because you are wrong. The next time you find yourself arguing, and somebody quotes Scripture to you, you had better back off. You have to realize that you are fighting the Word, and that's the same as fighting God.

The Pharisees tried to defend themselves. But Jesus put a noose around their neck and was about to jerk the slack out of them. This is what He said in verse 8:

> **Moses because of the hardness of your hearts suffered you to put away** (or to divorce) **your wives: but from the beginning it was not so.**

He was telling them that they couldn't get divorced for just any cause. The only reason God gave them a writing of divorcement was because they wouldn't yield to His Word in the first place. Because of the hardness of their heart and rebellion against God, Moses had to come up with some regulatory laws so that order could be put back in their lives.

Jesus was saying to them: "You have rebelled against God. You won't submit to Him and to His rules. You won't submit to His law of love. You won't let God work His will in your lives. Therefore, because you have gotten into sin through the hardness of your hearts and have rebelled against God, God will regulate it."

Now you have to understand who Jesus was speaking to here. He was dealing with one set of people, and they were covenant people. His answer about divorce was being spoken to those who today would be called believers. Look again at what He said in verse 8:

Moses because of the hardness of your hearts suffered you to put away your wives: but from the beginning it was not so.

He was saying to them: "You come here trying to defend your religion. If you really want the answer, I will tell you."

 # The Only Scriptural Reason for Divorce

In verse 9 He gave them the answer, but it wasn't what they really wanted to hear. The answer He gave has held us in check ever since. Verse 9:

> **And I say unto you, Whosoever shall put away** (or divorce) **his wife, except it be for fornication** (or sexual impurity), **and shall marry another, committeth adultery: and whoso marrieth her which is put away doth commit adultery.**

In regulating it, God tells us that there are scriptural reasons to get a divorce and that some divorces are approved in the sight of God. So, every divorce is not sinful, though sin was probably what caused it to happen.

That's why you can't judge every divorce situation in the same way. They aren't all equal.

Jesus was saying: "If you divorce your spouse for any reason other than fornication and sexual impurity, you enter into adultery; and anyone who marries that person enters into adultery."

The Disciples' Reaction

The disciples responded by saying to Him:

**If the case of the man be so with his
wife, it is not good to marry.**

Matthew 19:10

Why did the disciples react so strongly when He said that?

Because of the Law.

According to Leviticus 20:10, adultery was to be paid for with capital punishment, and both the man and woman involved would be stoned to death.

Deuteronomy 22:22 says that if a married woman and a single man engage in an adulterous affair, both of them will be put to death.

The disciples were saying: "Do You mean, Lord, that if I get divorced and put away my wife just because of incompatibility, I have entered into adultery? Wait a minute, Lord. If I do that, they have a legal right to take me out and stone me."

 ## Marriage and Divorce Are Serious!

What was the Lord saying here? Two things.

Number one, He wanted to get across to them the seriousness of marriage. It isn't something we should be jumping into lightly. It's something that God witnesses, and He will hold us accountable for it.

You aren't to marry somebody you wouldn't want to live with for the rest of your life, and you don't get married for fleshly reasons. You shouldn't marry just for any cause, because you can't get divorced just for any cause. When entering into the marriage covenant, you must be serious about it, because God holds you accountable. That's the first thing the Lord was saying.

Secondly, when Jesus said unscriptural divorce would bring adultery, which is a capital offense, did He mean that death and judgment would come to the people? I don't think so. Why not? We have to study the Scriptures a little deeper. It takes more than just surface reading.

First of all, if Jesus meant that this was adultery — the sexual act of impurity or sexual intercourse with someone other than the marriage partner — then why didn't He have the two women stoned who were living in adultery?

One of them was an adulteress caught by the scribes and Pharisees and brought before Jesus for judgment. (See John 8:3-11.) The other one was a Samaritan woman Jesus met at the well, who had been married five times and was living with another man at the time. (See John 4:15-26.)

But Jesus didn't have either of them stoned.

Apparently, the Lord didn't practice stoning, and that isn't really what He was trying to get across. He wasn't telling us that we should take people out and stone them. He was pointing out to us the seriousness of marriage and the seriousness of divorce.

The Full Meaning of Adultery

Now I want us to look at something here.

Adultery means the breaking of wedlock through sexual immorality. *Strong's Concordance* also gives a figurative meaning as that of apostasy.[1]

Apostasy means "to fall away from God, to break fellowship with God, to abandon one's faith or belief, literally, 'to stand away from in varying degrees.'"[2] It means to separate yourself from God or to pull away from Him.

Again, the Lord said in Matthew 19:9:

> **Whosoever shall put away his wife, except it be for fornication, and shall marry another, committeth adultery: and whoso marrieth her which is put away doth commit adultery.**

In this case, Jesus is saying that the husband is committing adultery and is causing his wife to commit adultery, too. He could actually be saying this:

If you don't divorce because sexual impurities have already happened, you are putting yourself into a place where you will fall away from God. You are hurting your own walk with God and are causing your wife to pull away from her walk with God. Anybody else who gets involved will be pulled away from God. As a result, the spiritual condition of all who are involved will be affected.

Could Jesus have been talking about such a situation? Yes. I believe that in this passage the Lord was dealing with spiritual things.

He was saying that the only scriptural reason two believers can get a divorce is for sexual impurity or unfaithfulness. Incompatibility is not a permissible reason for two believers to be divorced.

According to Deuteronomy 24:1, if a man marries a woman and finds something unclean about her, he would be allowed to divorce her. That doesn't mean he could find something about her personality that he didn't like. It's saying that, after a man marries a woman, if he finds that she has been doing him wrong by sleeping around on him, then he can divorce her.

When the Pharisees came to Jesus and asked if a man could be divorced for just any cause, they were thinking of something like incompatibility — for instance, the wife might have had a personality quirk, or maybe there was a problem with their in-laws.

But Jesus was saying to them: "You have to understand that if two believers form a marriage covenant together, the only recourse they have is for one of them to become unfaithful to that covenant through impurity or unfaithfulness. If one of them deals treacherously with the other, then they can turn to divorce as a remedy."

Now let's go further into this study by looking at the subject of spiritual adultery.

CHAPTER 9

Spiritual Adultery

I don't believe Jesus was just talking about the physical act of sexual impurity, but was dealing with a spiritual law. We can get some clearness of thought on this by looking in the gospel of Matthew.

Remember, apostasy is a tearing away or a pulling apart. It is falling away in various degrees and denying your faith and belief in God. I believe Jesus was actually taking us back to the Word. He was trying to show us that if a man decides to divorce his wife for just any cause, he would be bringing spiritual damage to himself, to his wife and to everybody involved in their situation. Let me prove this to you.

 # Apostasy in the Heart

In chapter 5 of Matthew's gospel, Jesus said:

> **Ye have heard that it was said by them of old time, Thou shalt not commit adultery:**
>
> **But I say unto you, That whosoever looketh on a woman to lust after her hath committed adultery with her already in his heart.**
>
> **Matthew 5:27,28**

Now He can't be talking here about the physical act of adultery. When saying that this man had committed adultery with her already in his heart, He must be talking about spiritual adultery.

In other words, He was saying: "You have committed apostasy in your heart. You have set your heart to be hard and have placed yourself in a position of rebellion against God's Word. By refusing to submit to God, you have put yourself in a position to get into sin, and that will cause great damage to come upon you."

I believe Jesus is talking about this, because He ties it together in verses 29 and 30 by saying:

> **And if thy right eye offend thee, pluck it out, and cast it from thee: for it is profitable for thee that one of thy members should perish, and not that thy whole body should be cast into hell.**

> **And if thy right hand offend thee, cut it off, and cast it from thee: for it is profitable for thee that one of thy members should perish, and not that thy whole body should be cast into hell.**

Is He saying that if we have problems with our right hand, we should take an axe and chop it off? Or is He telling us that if we can't keep from looking at pornographic material, we should stick a finger behind our eyeball and just pull it out?

I don't think so.

I believe Jesus was talking here about spiritual law because He was dealing with the heart. Remember in Malachi 2:16 God said, **Take heed to your spirit** (or your heart). So Jesus is saying:

"In the old time, adultery was an act of the flesh. But now you need to realize that, under the New Covenant, the heart is going to govern man, so you need to take heed to your heart.

"If you begin to look lustfully, you will allow that lust down into your heart, and to be lustful is the opposite of having faith in God. Therefore, you will be lusting after the flesh instead of seeking after the things of God. You will be allowing apostasy, or spiritual adultery, to take place within you."

Say *No!* to Lust

No matter how you may be letting lust into your life — whether it's through your eyes or through your hands or through your thoughts — you need to do what Romans 8:13 says: mortify the deeds of the flesh by the Spirit.

You have to take in God's Word, allowing it to wash and cleanse and purge you until you are set free from those lustful thoughts and desires.

If you can't stop watching dirty movies, then get rid of your TV and your VCR. You have to spend time in the Word to clean up your act. If you don't do that, you will be thrown into rebellion and sin, and eventually destruction will come into your life.

So, whatever sinful desire may be rising up within you, cut it off. Be like a new convert.

You can't be going back right away into that old way of life which you were delivered out of when you got saved. Don't be trying to go back around sinners to witness to them about Jesus. You aren't strong enough to do that yet.

If you go back into the bar, you will drink. If you go back to the drug house, you will get high. You will be led right back into sexual promiscuity.

You need to cut yourself off from those old ways. Why? Because there will be a temptation to be pulled back into that sin.

So what is the Lord saying? Take heed to your heart. Be on guard. Watch out. Don't allow lust to get into any area of your life. Cut it off. Mortify it. Don't have anything to do with it. Put it to death.

 ## Another Example of Apostasy

Then in Matthew 5:31,32 Jesus deals with divorce and adultery again. He says:

> **It hath been said, Whosoever shall put away his wife, let him give her a writing of divorcement:**
>
> **But I say unto you, That whosoever shall put away his wife, saving for the cause of fornication, causeth her to commit adultery: and whosoever shall marry her that is divorced committeth adultery.**

Here it is again: Jesus' statement of the fact that there is only one legal reason for two believers to be divorced: if there is fornication on the part of one or both of them. He says that if divorce occurs for any other reason, then they have committed adultery.

Now He can't be talking about the sexual act of adultery, or the physical act of sex. How do I know? Because this verse says the husband causes the wife to commit adultery at the point of divorce. Let's read this again. Verse 32:

But I say unto you, That whosoever shall put away his wife, saving for the cause of fornication, causeth her to commit adultery....

This doesn't say it causes the wife to commit adultery once she joins with another man. It says the moment the husband puts her away, the moment their divorce is enacted for any reason other than fornication, he causes her to commit adultery right then.

But how could she have committed adultery at that point? I thought it required another person to be involved.

It does. That means Jesus can't be talking about the act of sexual impurity, or that the wife had intercourse with another man. She hasn't had time to do anything like that.

So what is He talking about here? Again, He is talking about apostasy. So we have to apply the full definition and read it in context as to what He is saying.

You see, if fornication has already taken place, then there has already been a pulling away, a falling away. The marriage vows have already been broken.

But if nothing has happened between the husband and wife to cause a falling away or a tearing apart, and they are divorced, then they have caused apostasy (a falling away or a tearing apart) to occur between them. He rips her from himself, and she is apostate at that point. She has fallen away in a varying degree by being pulled down and torn apart from him.

You need to understand something about divorce: Whether it's easy or whether it's hard, divorce will always cause some damage.

What God Joins, Man Separates

As we have already established, marriage is a spiritual covenant between a husband and a wife, who come together and become one in their hearts. But they don't become one physically at that point.

So why does the Bible say they become one flesh?

Because God sees them as operating together in all of life's ways and life's situations. They become one — spirit and soul and body.

It was God Who joined them together. As it says in First Corinthians 6, believers are joined to the Lord and become one spirit with Him. The same is true in marriage. When the husband and wife are joined together, they become one spirit and are to be in agreement, in one accord.

That doesn't mean they lose their separate identities and are no longer two individuals. But in the marriage covenant, they are one with God and one with each other.

Now, the Lord is saying this: When you allow divorce for any reason other than an act of fornication, you are basically reaching into your spouse and separating what God has put together. As Scripture says, **What therefore God hath joined together, let not man put asunder** (Matt. 19:6). Only man can separate what God has joined together.

What God puts together is perfect; what man takes apart is imperfect. When God puts the woman with the man, they become one spirit; and, in the eyes of God, they are joined perfectly together. But when divorce takes place, man separates what God had formed. God had put it together well; man just ripped it apart.

If you were to take a piece of paper and rip it apart, that paper wouldn't tear in a straight line so that it could easily be put back together again. Instead, there would be jagged edges.

Well, the Lord is saying that whenever a husband (or wife) pushes to get a divorce for any reason other than adultery, he is causing adultery, or apostasy, to take place in her, and he is tearing himself from her.

When they became husband and wife, they were joined together. God made them one, and they were fit perfectly together. But then when the divorce was enacted, man ripped apart what God had put together.

It happened like this: They began by having a hard time in their relationship with God; then their relationship with each other was torn apart, and their spirits were wounded. As a result, she took a little from him and he took a little from her; then they both were left torn and jagged. And their kids were seriously affected by it.

The Results of Marrying a Divorced Person

Again quoting Matthew 5:32, Jesus says:

> **...and whosoever shall marry her that is divorced committeth adultery.**

How is it that another man commits adultery by marrying the woman who had been divorced from her first husband?

It might happen something like this:

The spirit of that woman was ripped and torn all to pieces when she was separated from her husband. It hurt her walk with God and with their kids. Then when another man came into her life and meshed with her, he joined himself with the rips and tears that had been left in her spirit. So, there was some serious damage that had to be healed.

At some point, those two have to let God mold them together. They have to let Him clean out the rips, heal the hurts and remove all the torn pieces that were left from the old marriage and are still hanging on.

So what is Jesus talking about regarding divorce? Is He just talking about sexual immorality and how someone should be stoned to death as a result? No. I believe He is talking about damage that occurs in the heart.

Now do you see why God hates divorce? Do you see why the Lord Jesus Christ was putting such emphasis on it when the Pharisees came and asked Him about it? Do you see why He wouldn't waver and boldly told them what the Word said about it?

That brings us to a question the religious church asks all the time: "Well, if you marry a divorced woman, then are you living in adultery with her?" No. If you came together and if God put you together, then you aren't living in physical adultery.

But there is something you will enter into when you marry a divorced person, and that is all the excess garbage that came out of that last marriage; all the hurt, anger, frustration and mistrust that was left in that damaged spirit. You will have to deal with all of that. If you have been there, you know I am telling the absolute truth.

That's the adultery Jesus was talking about and warning about.

If you are faced with it now, you might ask, "How am I going to deal with it?"

By letting God take care of it and healing all the hurt and pain within you.

You know, it's even gotten to the point that some people say: "Well, if a man gets remarried, then every time he has sex with his wife, he will have to get down on his knees, repent and ask God to forgive him for committing adultery with her." That's stupid!

If he did get remarried feeling that way, he wouldn't be able to have a good sexual relationship with his wife. Every time they had sex, he would think he had actually committed a sinful, adulterous act. He would stay bound up and hindered all through life.

But Jesus wasn't just talking about the physical act; He was talking about the spiritual damage that takes place when someone goes through a divorce. He was pointing out that healing is needed.

I have watched people who have remarried still not have the relationship they should have had after ten or fifteen years. They still have some jagged edges from the past, and they need to let God knock that off. But it can only happen when they get into the Word of God and let the Lord really do a work in them, bringing victory and healing into their spirit.

After a Divorce, Either Remain Unmarried or Be Reconciled

Now let's look again in First Corinthians, chapter 7. Paul is talking here to the husband or wife of a believer. He says:

**And unto the married I command, yet
not I, but the Lord, Let not the wife depart
from** (or divorce) **her husband:**

**But and if she depart, let her remain
unmarried, or be reconciled to her husband: and let not the husband put away** (or
divorce) **his wife.**

1 Corinthians 7:10,11

What is Paul saying here?

If both the husband and wife are Christians, they have
only one reason to get a divorce: because one of them has
been unfaithful to the other by committing fornication or
acts of sexual immorality. Either the husband or the wife
has broken their covenant and the vows they had made to
one another.

Now if they don't have that as a reason for divorce, but
they just can't get along, then Paul is saying to them: "Okay,
you can get a divorce, but you have to stay unmarried or be
reconciled to that person."

Now why does he say for them to stay unmarried?
Because he doesn't want them getting themselves into more
of a mess than they were before.

If both of them are believers, it's possible that they could pray and repent of their strife with one another and their rebellion against God. Then there is a good chance that the two of them could get back together, salvage their marriage and go on with God through life. But regardless of whether they are reconciled, they still are living under the law of love, and love says they must forgive. (Matt. 6:14,15; Mark 11:25,26.)

If a husband and wife are believers, and the wife commits adultery, can the husband just get rid of her? Not if she repents and comes back, wanting their marriage to be restored. The Bible says he has to forgive and take her back.

That's when believers will find out just how much they really want to submit to the Lord. You see, God is looking for reconciliation. He wants to see those two get back together again.

So, believers have to submit to God and to His Word. They have to start letting the Word work in them by submitting to the law of love and letting God begin to build a foundation in their lives.

They may realize that their marriage was a mistake and

decide to get divorced; but if they do, they will have to stay unmarried. Otherwise, they would be breaking God's laws.

Wrong Reasons for Divorce

God is saying: "Don't just get divorced so that you can find someone better."

Some Christians might say, "Well, we don't get along, and we didn't really have anything in common when we were married." But they should have thought of that before they got married.

Others might say, "Well, it was really a physical affair that caused us to get married."

They shouldn't have been sexually involved before they got married. Six months after their wedding, it won't be as much fun to them as it was when they were out sneaking around!

Divorce Between the Believer and the Unbeliever

Now let's see what Scripture says about this next subject: divorce between the believer and the unbeliever.

Continuing in First Corinthians 7, verse 12, the apostle Paul writes:

But to the rest speak I, not the Lord....

Now you might ask, "Does this mean Paul was writing by permission of the Lord?"

If you study this in context, you will see that this is what Paul was saying: "When the Lord Jesus was here, He didn't address this subject; He only addressed it between believers."

As we have seen in Matthew 19, Jesus was dealing with covenant people. He was not asked the question concerning believers and unbelievers because at the time He was dealing only with believers. So Paul was saying, "I am speaking in behalf of the Lord." In other words, he was saying, "If the Lord were here, this is what He would say."

That means this is just as much law and just as inspired as if Jesus Himself had laid it out when He was here. So what is the Lord saying?

But to the rest speak I, not the Lord: If any brother hath a wife that believeth not, and she be pleased to dwell with him, let

him not put her away.

1 Corinthians 7:12

In other words, if the husband is a believer who is married to an unbeliever, and she loves him and is trying to make a go of their marriage, then divorce would not be allowed just because she is an unbeliever.

Verse 13 says:

And the woman which hath an husband that believeth not, and if he be pleased to dwell with her, let her not leave him.

Just because a woman who is a believer is married to a man who is not a believer, that's no reason for her to divorce him.

For the unbelieving husband is sanctified by the wife, and the unbelieving wife is sanctified by the husband: else were your children unclean; but now are they holy.

But if the unbelieving depart, let him depart. A brother or a sister is not under

> **bondage in such cases: but God hath called us to peace.**
>
> **1 Corinthians 7:14,15**

The last word here in verse 15 is the key: **God hath called us to** *peace.*

Now what are the rules that go along with this?

To Christian men and women who are married to unbelievers, it says that they should be pleased to dwell with their spouse. Their unbelieving spouse may truly love them and be trying to do right as their partner in life. If the only disagreement between them is about their walk with Christ, God is telling believers: "Stay with your unbelieving spouse."

Believers are to do what First Peter 3 says and love their spouse. Unbelievers will be won over by the love which they see and receive, as their spouse just keeps walking with God and praying over them. In this way God will be able to bless their home and their children, and there will be a certain amount of peace in that home. God can also put protection over unbelieving spouses until they are saved. There will be hope for God to move in their lives.

Now what does it mean if the husband is not pleased to dwell with his wife? It means that she has been unfaithful to him. On the other hand, suppose the husband is abusing his wife. Let's say he comes home and treats her badly by slapping her around or beating her down with his words. In either situation, whether husband or wife, they are not pleased about having to live in a situation like that, and there is no peace in their lives.

God says that if you are being bombarded in such a way, if your marriage is a struggle and you have done all you know to do, then you can divorce that person. It says you are not under bondage. That means you would be free to get married again and to go on with God. But remarriage would be allowed only after you have been healed and your relationship with Christ has been restored.

A Real Believer Must Act Like One

You might say: "I was married to this guy, who professed to be a Christian, but he cussed and had temper tantrums. He beat me up and wouldn't provide for the family."

Are you sure he was really a believer?

"Well, he said he was a Christian. He went to church and sang out loud during all those church services."

I want you to realize that, first of all, a believer is supposed to act like one.

If two people are calling themselves believers and one of them is acting like an unbeliever, that one has to be judged as an unbeliever. If he isn't a believer, that means he's a sinner!

Righteous Judgment

Now we have already established that marriage is a covenant between a husband and a wife. God put them together. He expects them to keep the vows they made to one another and to live out their lives with one another. They are to have true companionship, sharing and working with each other, raising up godly children and being blessed as their prayers are answered and God prospers them. That's what God created marriage to be.

Divorce, on the other hand, is the dissolving of that covenant. A husband and wife are separated and pulled from each other, and they have to go back into life as an unmarried, or single, person.

Now, as we have learned, there is such a thing as scriptural divorce. It occurs in a situation when both husband and wife are Christians, but one falls away from God and gets off into error. He or she stops doing what they know to do. They can be saying, "Hallelujah," in church and be living just like the devil at home. A person who is a hypocrite cannot really be looked upon as a Christian.

People like this are struggling spiritually. They don't want to go to church. They don't want to read the Bible. They don't want to act in any way like a Christian. So, they have to be judged as an unbeliever.

God says that if unbelievers are not pleased to dwell with believers, giving of themselves and fulfilling their marriage covenant, then they must face righteous judgment. First Corinthians 6:1,2 says that believers are not to go before the law of unbelievers; they are to bring their problem before the leadership of the church and have it judged.

After hearing the situation, the pastor and elders of the church will judge what was right and what was wrong, who was right and who was wrong; then they will render a righteous verdict.

Let's say a husband and wife come before me as their pastor, with both of them saying they are a Christian. If the husband has been unfaithful to his wife, their situation can automatically be judged. He is in adultery; and if he doesn't want to have their marriage restored, then she would be free to divorce and to go on with her life.

But what if he isn't unfaithful to her? What if he is mentally abusive to her and won't do what the Word says by providing for her and being the priest of their home? Then he must be exposed for what he is.

As his pastor, I would say to him: "You don't have the right to beat down and slander and destroy this woman. Either you will be the kind of husband to her that's described in God's Word, or she will be rendered the proper right and judgment from the church to divorce you and to go on with God."

A Time of Restoration

Now, the judgment would come down to this: After the divorce is allowed, the wife can't just go out and immediately get married again.

First, she must allow time for her spiritual relationship with God to be fully restored and for her own spirit to be healed. Then she must give her husband time to repent and to restore himself unto the Lord, allowing God the opportunity to reconcile them.

If he stays away, refusing God and refusing to change, while she goes on with God and allows her wounds to be healed, God may bring another man across her path somewhere down the line. When that happens, her former husband has missed out on the opportunity to win her back. He can't wait until God brings somebody else across her path before he shows up in church, expecting her to just take him back. That wouldn't be acceptable.

This would be the scriptural method of judging such a situation. You see, God is not wanting to bring us into bondage and defeat.

Now let's consider the subject of unscriptural divorce.

CHAPTER 10

Unscriptural Divorce

What would be an unscriptural divorce? I will tell you.

Unscriptural divorce occurs between two Christians. They may love God, read their Bibles and be involved in church; but because they haven't applied the law of love and developed a real relationship with one another, they drift apart. They say, "After spending these years together, we just aren't compatible, and we never really had anything in common; so we want a divorce."

That man and that woman are supposed to be believers, so they have to submit themselves to God and let Him begin to do some things in their lives. They should be kneeling down at the altar and praying until the fire of God comes back into them. It can take that hard heart out of them and replace it with a heart of love. Then they will be able to start expressing that love to one another.

You see, it's just too easy for God's people to decide to give up on marriage when they say, "We aren't compatible, and we don't have anything in common." The truth is, they don't really want to work at it.

So that would be an unscriptural divorce. When a man and woman are divorced for such a reason, I wouldn't recommend that they ever get remarried.

Love Requires Some Action

The husband might say, "I don't love her anymore," or the wife might say, "I don't love him anymore." But love is not a feeling. Love is a decision based on the Word of God. According to First John 2:5, love is developed and perfected by acting on the Word of God.

I love my wife, Bonnie, and she loves me. But if we were to go several months without expressing our love to one another, in just a few more months, we would feel like strangers. We wouldn't have much in common.

Love requires some action. The apostle John said, **My little children, let us not love in word, neither in tongue; but in deed and in truth** (1 John 3:18). Love won't work without corresponding actions.

Divorce Is Sin, But God Forgives

Somebody might ask, "But if God hates divorce, then how does He feel about the person who has been divorced?"

Let's look once again in First Corinthians, chapter 6, beginning in verse 9:

> **Know ye not that the unrighteous shall not inherit the kingdom of God? Be not deceived: neither fornicators, nor idolaters, nor adulterers, nor effeminate, nor abusers of themselves with mankind,**
>
> **Nor thieves, nor covetous, nor drunkards, nor revilers, nor extortioners, shall inherit the kingdom of God.**
>
> **And such were some of you: but ye are washed, but ye are sanctified, but ye are**

**justified in the name of the Lord Jesus,
and by the Spirit of our God.**

1 Corinthians 6:9-11

What is the apostle Paul saying here? That divorce is no worse than any of the other sins listed in this passage of Scripture.

If God can cleanse you and wash you from all these other sins, He can forgive you of divorce. Divorce is not the unpardonable sin. God can forgive you and give you life after divorce. That's been proven. We will deal with this more when we look into the subject of remarriage.

Divorce and Adultery

Let's look again at the Scripture where Jesus was dealing with divorce and adultery:

**But I say unto you, That whosoever
shall put away his wife, saving for the
cause of fornication, causeth her to commit adultery: and whosoever shall marry
her that is divorced committeth adultery.**

Matthew 5:32

As we have already seen, Jesus was talking here about more than adultery in just the physical sense.

But whether adultery was spiritual or physical, is it a forgivable offense? Yes, it is. As was mentioned before, adultery is not the unpardonable sin.

Apparently, when faced with the problem of divorce among believers, the Lord is more interested in forgiving them and allowing them to go on with life than in condemning them for their actions.

As was referred to in a previous chapter, John's gospel reveals Jesus' dealings with two women of adultery.

When He was talking with the woman whom He met at the well, it was revealed to Him that she had been divorced five times and was living with another man. But He didn't condemn her for it. In fact, He ministered to her that He was the Messiah, and it changed her life. She even went on to become an evangelist by going into town and telling everybody that He was the Messiah. That means God can use even a divorced person. (John 4:15-30.)

Then there was the adulteress brought to Him by the scribes and Pharisees, who asked Him if she should be stoned. He didn't recommend stoning as judgment for her sin; but, instead, He spoke the truth to her, saying, "I do not condemn you; go, and sin no more," and she was set free from that bondage. (John 8:3-11.)

Apparently, Jesus was more interested in those two sinners being forgiven than in their being called an adulteress for the rest of their lives.

Today, Jesus is saying to those who have divorced and remarried: "Don't make the same mistakes in this marriage that you made in your first one. Repent and allow your heart to be healed. Get your life straightened out; then go on with God."

You need to receive what the Bible says and act the way Jesus did toward the sin of adultery. If it's physical adultery, God can forgive and heal all the hurts that have come as a result. Even if it's spiritual adultery — apostasy, a falling away, a tearing apart — God can still heal the broken heart. Jesus said that's why He came: **The Spirit of the Lord is upon me, because...he hath sent me to heal the brokenhearted** (Luke 4:18).

 # Divorce and Remarriage

Now, here's a question that comes up regarding divorce: If a man and woman get divorced, are they really divorced in God's eyes, or are they still considered married to one another?

In some churches, any person who gets divorced is seen as still being legally married to their spouse.

Let me give you the answers that were given by both Jesus and the apostle Paul. Then my question to you is: Will you believe them?

Jesus' Attitude Toward Divorce

I want us to look now at Jesus' conversation with the woman at the well, only this time in more detail.

Let's begin in John, chapter 4, verse 16:

> **Jesus saith unto her, Go, call thy husband, and come hither.**
>
> **The woman answered and said, I have no husband.**

Now is she lying or telling the truth? Let's find out.

Jesus said unto her, Thou hast well said, I have no husband (v. 17).

In other words, Jesus was saying to her, "You're telling Me the truth; you don't have a husband."

Now notice the next part of Jesus' words to her. In verse 18 He says:

For thou hast had five husbands; and he whom thou now hast is not thy husband: in that saidst thou truly.

According to Jesus, this woman had been married five times but wasn't married anymore. When she had said, "I don't have a husband," Jesus had responded: "You're right, and what you're saying is true: You *don't* have a husband. You have been married five times and divorced five times, and the man you're living with now isn't your husband. You are living in sin, but you are not married."

So, the Lord Jesus is clearly saying that the person who gets divorced is *not married.*

 # Paul's View of Divorce

Now let's see what the apostle Paul has to say in First Corinthians, chapter 7. Verse 11 says:

> **But and if she depart** (meaning "gets a divorce"), **let her remain unmarried.**

The word *unmarried* simply means "not married," doesn't it? So, according to the apostle Paul, a person who gets a divorce is not married to the person he or she has divorced. It's just that simple.

Divorce Ends the Marriage Covenant

You need to thoroughly understand what divorce means: Divorce is the act of dissolving, tearing apart, putting away and absolutely finishing off the marriage covenant that was made between the man and the woman. As Jesus said in Matthew 19, it is putting asunder, separating or taking apart that which had been put together.

The enforcing of the divorce process brings to an end the marriage covenant which the husband and wife had entered into together. They had promised to provide companionship for one another, with all the responsibilitics and benefits thereof. Divorce has now terminated all requirements and responsibilities of those involved and all the privileges they shared with one another.

Now some religious people would say, "Well, they might be divorced, but we still count them as being married."

But let's think about this for a moment.

If they are divorced in law but not in God's eyes, that would mean they are still married and obligated to one another. The husband could be running around and doing his own thing; then anytime he wanted, he could just go back to his wife. He would be able to move back in with her, taking all his dirty laundry with him. He could have sex with her whenever he liked, and she would be obligated to comply.

Is that really the way God intended it to be? I don't think so.

Jesus, Who is God Incarnate, said that when a man and woman are divorced, they are *not married.* The apostle Paul, writing under the inspiration of the Holy Ghost, said they are *unmarried.* That means they are no longer married, either in God's eyes or in the Law's eyes.

That's what divorce really means: becoming unmarried, or single, again. It is the separating and dissolving of the marriage covenant.

So in answer to some religious people's idea that in God's eyes a divorced couple is still married to one another, my answer to them is emphatically, *No, they aren't!*

As a result of divorce, the man and woman are released from the vows they had spoken to one another. They will no longer be held accountable for the obligations they had made to one another or the responsibilities they had accepted for one another. But neither will they be allowed the privileges they had given to one another. They can no longer be one flesh, because they have split apart that which had been put together. The two of them are no longer one but have been separated, and each of them will be allowed to go their own way.

CHAPTER 11

What About Remarriage?

Let's find out now what the apostle Paul has to say about remarriage. First of all, he deals with the widow.

Remarriage for the Widow

> **The wife is bound by the law as long as her husband liveth; but if her husband be dead, she is at liberty to be married to whom she will; only in the Lord.**
>
> **1 Corinthians 7:39**

Paul is saying that the widow is at liberty to remarry whomever she will, but *only in the Lord.* In other words, she must marry a believer.

In First Timothy, chapter 5, Paul is speaking about widows; and in verse 14 he deals specifically with younger widows. He tells them that they ought to get married again, have babies, guide the home and live for God. They still have sexual wants and desires; and if they don't satisfy those needs, they might turn away from God, get off into sin and then find themselves in a mess.

Christian women who are widows always go through a time of hurt and grief and pain. They have to be healed by God; then they can continue on in their walk with Him. Once their past is behind them, God could lead them to get married once again.

When should a widow start thinking about remarriage?

Once her heart has been healed, she will begin to feel that she is ready to have a relationship with another man. Then God will say that it is acceptable for her to get remarried.

Now the religious world doesn't take any pity on the widow or widower. In the eyes of some churches, those who get remarried are seen as having committed adultery against their first spouse who had gone on to be with the Lord.

But the marriage pledge ends with the vow: "Till death do us part." Jesus said of the life to come:

For when they shall rise from the dead, they neither marry, nor are given in marriage; but are as the angels which are in heaven.

Mark 12:25

In other words, marriage is not part of life in heaven. Once marriage partners die and leave the earth, their marriage no longer exists. So, marriage is an experience of life intended only for this side of heaven.

As Paul has said, as long as the husband is alive, the wife is bound to him; but when he has died, she is free to marry again. In other words, that marriage is over, and the widow is allowed to marry whomever she wills, but only in the Lord. We need to establish that truth in our hearts.

Looking Further Into Remarriage

Now, let's look closer at the subject of remarriage and see what the Word says about it.

When the Pharisees asked Jesus a question about divorce, He responded by asking them, **Have ye not read...?** (Matt. 19:4). So, if you want to find some answers, go to the Word. The Lord always guides us to the Word.

In First Corinthians, chapter 7, Paul wrote:

> **Art thou bound unto a wife? seek not to be loosed. Art thou loosed from a wife? seek not a wife** (v. 27).

What binds a husband to his wife? The marriage vows he made to her in the beginning. But, according to this verse, he can be loosed from his wife.

The word *loosed* in the Greek means divorced.[1] In other words, he can be loosed from those vows he made when they were married.

God is saying to husbands, "If you are divorced from your wife, don't go seeking another one." In other words, you don't just get divorced from one woman so that you can have another. You see, the Bible is explicitly clear about divorcing somebody so that you can run off and marry somebody else. God doesn't smile favorably on that at all.

Seek God First

Well, if I'm divorced, why am I not allowed to seek a spouse?

Because you are to seek God first.

Can I ever get remarried?

Look at the next verse:

> **But and if thou marry, thou hast not sinned....**
>
> **1 Corinthians 7:28**

Paul is talking here about remarriage for those who were loosed from their spouse. Notice it is saying that if you have divorced and then have remarried, you have not sinned. Why? Because you didn't get a divorce so that you could go and marry somebody else. When you were divorced, you began to seek God, not another spouse. Then God brought somebody else to you down the line, and it all worked out.

Paul is saying that when you were remarried, your remarriage was not a sin. Now that really throws a wrinkle in our thinking, doesn't it? It seems that remarriage has been made to be absolutely the most ungodly and worst sin that anybody could ever commit. But, according to Paul, it isn't sin.

Be Willing To Receive Counsel

But what if two professing Christians want to be divorced because they just aren't getting along? Then it requires some righteous judgment by the leadership of their church. The trouble is, the pastors in most churches aren't qualified to judge it, because they don't have any idea about what to do.

So how should it be judged when adultery isn't involved? Their pastor needs to spend time counseling with them.

In First Corinthians 6:1,2 Paul is asking, "Why would believers go to unbelievers to have their marriage judged?" They shouldn't just go to their lawyers and get a divorce. First, they should sit down with their pastor and tell him how they feel.

Both of them didn't just wake up one morning and say, "Well, praise God, it's God's will that we get a divorce today!" Somewhere down the line, something went wrong, and it began with hardness of heart. Maybe one of them allowed lust to get in and adultery to take place in the heart.

When they begin to talk about their situation, the pastor should immediately be able to recognize who has hardness of heart. One of them is rebelling against God and wants the divorce. It would be up to the pastor to find out who is responsible for what.

Now let's say that they both repent to their pastor. But they don't want to do what the Word says and obey God's law of love. They still want a divorce and are determined to get one. Then because of that decision, they are granted permission by their pastor to divorce.

But as we have read in First Corinthians 7, verses 10 and 11, if these two born-again believers get a divorce, they must either remain unmarried or be reconciled.

Both of them continue to attend church after the divorce; and, as the Bible says, he is not to seek a wife and she is not to seek a husband. Now they can fellowship with others; but they aren't to go out and start dating, looking to find another person to be their spouse. It's up to them to get their hearts right with God by totally selling out to Him.

If their pastor is working with them, and the church is trying to get them reconciled, one of them may begin to yield and say, "Well, I didn't really want the divorce anyway." That person then begins to pursue God and to do right, even wanting to get back with the spouse; but maybe the other one still doesn't want it.

So what does the pastor have to do? He has to judge the situation. But how does he judge it?

Let's say it's the husband who doesn't want to get involved again. A certain amount of time has lapsed, and the pastor has given him time to repent. But with hardness of heart, he has turned against God's Word.

As Matthew 18:15-17 says, the pastor must offer him counsel and try to get him straightened out and right with God again. The man even gets brought before the church leadership, but he doesn't want to receive their counsel. So the pastor has no other option than to judge him as an unbeliever.

The apostle Paul did that. He said a person who rejects counsel and rejects God should not be given fellowship, but should be marked and dealt with as an unbeliever. (Rom. 16:17.)

Such a person should be seen as an unbelieving believer, or one who is not a Christian. If it's the husband, then the wife can be told that she is free of him and would be allowed to get married again if she chooses.

Now suppose God brings some other man across her path who will love her and care for her. If her husband is still being a rascal and is rebelling against God, with hardness of heart, she wouldn't be sinning to get married a second time. God would allow that. So remarriage is fine in that kind of situation.

You have to judge it that way. It's really simple. You find out who is willing to do what God says and who isn't. The one who is willing will be blessed by God; the one who refuses God will suffer the consequences.

Let's say the husband and wife have some problems. He does wrong, and she gets hurt over it. Even though he acted a mess, he still wants to live for God, so he repents and begins to act right. He does everything he can to win her back, but she has become hardened toward him and still won't have him. If she finds somebody else and gets married again, her remarriage must be judged as wrong. But, as a result, he then is free to marry again if he chooses to do so.

That is righteous judgment. In that case, as the Bible says, they have married but have not sinned.

Be Released By God To Remarry

Again, First Corinthians 7:10,11 says that the believers who divorce are to remain unmarried or be reconciled.

You might ask, "How long should I wait before getting married again?"

Until God releases you or until reconciliation is no longer an option.

"What do you mean 'until God releases me'?"

Until you feel in your heart that you are released.

Until love for your spouse and a desire to be reconciled are no longer a part of you, or until reconciliation is impossible because your spouse has either backslidden or has married somebody else.

In any case, you know in your spirit that God has released you and set you free; therefore, you can go on with your life.

But before you would make the decision to marry again, you should place your situation before the leadership of your church and receive righteous judgment. The pastor and elders should then express their ruling by putting it in writing, something like this:

"Having researched this situation and having dealt with both parties, we have judged that she is forgiven, is clean and has a legal right to get remarried. Therefore, we are with her and for her. If God should bring another believer into her life, we would be willing to put our blessings upon their union."

Once this judgment has been documented, you would be able to go from there to unite in marriage with another believer. That's the way God and the apostle Paul said it should be handled, and the way today's pastors should be dealing with it.

CHAPTER 12

Can the Divorced Person Who Remarries Still Be Used in Ministry?

If I had been divorced and now am remarried, can I still be used by God in ministry and be a part of leadership in the Church?

This may sound like a tough question, but it really isn't. It has been answered right in the Scriptures.

God Has a Plan

Romans 11:29 says, **For the gifts and calling of God are without repentance.** This verse in the *New King James Version* reads: **For the gifts and the calling of God are**

irrevocable. That means God has a plan for each of us, and He wants so much to carry out that plan in our lives.

Let's look again in John, chapter 4, at the woman of Samaria who talked with Jesus at the well. Remember, she had five husbands and was living with another man. But then after Jesus cleansed her of that sinful life, Scripture says she went into town and told everybody about Him.

> **The woman then left her waterpot, and went her way into the city, and saith to the men,**
>
> **Come, see a man, which told me all things that ever I did: is not this the Christ?**
>
> **John 4:28,29**

Many believed on the Lord Jesus Christ because of the word of that woman. Look now at verse 39:

> **And many of the Samaritans of that city believed on him for the saying of the woman, which testified, He told me all that ever I did.**

So apparently the Lord used that woman in ministry,

even after she had lived such a life of sin, having been divorced and remarried five times.

Now I want us to look at some things the Lord has shown us in His Word.

God Will Forgive

First of all, we need to understand that forgiveness is sought through repentance. First John 1:9 says, **If we confess our sins, he** (God) **is faithful and just to forgive us our sins, and to cleanse us from all unrighteousness.**

I want you to realize that divorce is a sin, but not all divorce is sinful.

A person who has experienced divorce has been through a hurtful situation. But when the person who took part in that sin asks God for forgiveness, what does God do? He forgives. If that person repents, what happens? God cleanses him or her of that sin. And if God had His hand upon that person before, then He can still use him or her.

So it comes down to this: If God forgives you for making a mistake in your life, then shouldn't the Church do the same?

 # Qualifications for Leadership

According to First Timothy 3, verses 1-11, the apostle Paul gives qualifications for leadership in the Church.

Now somebody will come along about now and take Scripture out of context and quote verse 2, which says:

A bishop then must be blameless, the husband of one wife.

That person will then say, "See there, it says God's ministers are to have only one wife. That means if they have remarried, then they would have two spouses!"

But we have already established that, once divorced, a man is no longer married to that woman.

If you want more proof, do a little research on the Greek wording. Now I'm not a Greek scholar, but I can read what Greek scholars have said. The Greek word used here for the phrase *one wife* means "one wife at a time," not "married one time only."[1]

He said the church leaders were to be married to only one woman. He was trying to get rid of the idea that a man could have more than one wife. He wanted church leaders who were married to only one person at a time.

Now he wasn't talking about someone who was married and had never been divorced. He was saying of their leaders, "They must be married to only one person right now."

When I was studying this and thinking about it, I noticed that he had mentioned some of the qualifications of their leaders. Verse 7:

> **Moreover he must have a good report**
> **of them which are without; lest he fall into**
> **reproach and the snare of the devil.**

Let's say a man was in sin and went through an unscriptural divorce that was a real mess. It caused lots of problems, and the families were all split up. Then acting against the rules of the Church, he got remarried. But he reached the point that he was willing to repent in the sight of God, so God forgave him for all that mess. Now he still had the moral obligation to deal with the parties he had damaged, but he was forgiven in the sight of God.

In spite of all the terrible things that man had done, can God still bless the marriage he entered into through rebellion and sin? Certainly He can. I have already shown you some illustrations of that.

Should the Church forgive him for what he had done? Yes — even if it was a mess. What he had done could have been so ungodly and so against the Word that it might turn our stomachs to hear about it. But it isn't our place to judge him.

I am sure that in Old Testament days people were upset to learn what David had done to Bathsheba's husband in order to marry her. It was so bad that the prophet Nathan walked into the king's palace and rebuked David, telling him what would happen as the result of God's judgment upon him. (See 2 Sam. 11:2-27; 12:1-14.)

A terrible situation occurred in the lives of David and Bathsheba as the result of their sin, but God still blessed them when they repented and turned back to Him.

As Scripture says, the gifts and calling of God are irrevocable. So, when a person is called by God to be involved in leadership, he is to fulfill that calling, even though he may have made a real mess of his life. He has to turn back to God and ask for forgiveness and restoration as David did;

then God will receive him again. And if God forgives him, then his brothers and sisters in the Lord have to forgive him, too.

Reputation Must Be Rebuilt

Now, here's something you need to understand: The act of remarriage does not disqualify a person from being a leader in the church.

There would, however, be a certain period of time when that person would be disqualified. Because his reputation has been soiled, he wouldn't qualify to be a leader. Not because he wouldn't fit First Corinthians 7, but because he doesn't fit First Timothy 3, verse 7: He doesn't have a good report; or, in other words, a good reputation among others.

Then how long will that person have to stay out of leadership?

Until he and his spouse prove themselves by seeking God, staying humble and fighting through all of the junk that they created for themselves.

Until he rebuilds his reputation of integrity and honesty, and people will begin to look at him differently and have a different opinion of him.

Now that will take him some time. It might take one year. It might take five years. It might take fifteen or twenty years. It might take him the rest of his life. It just depends on how big a mess he has made.

But he is not disqualified for being a leader simply because he was divorced and has remarried. He is disqualifying himself as a leader so that he can take time to rebuild his reputation. Until he rebuilds the integrity and reputation of his life and of his heart towards God, people won't be willing to follow him.

Example of Time Spent Rebuilding

Let's say it was ten years ago when a church leader messed up by going totally against everything God had said in the Word. Maybe there was an ungodly divorce and an ungodly remarriage. No doubt the whole situation was unscriptural. But then he reached the point where he repented and turned back to God.

He and his wife have spent the last ten years weathering all the accusations against them and all the fuss they had created, in order to get themselves healed by God. They have fought through the storm and have dealt with the problems that had arisen. During these years they have grown and matured, staying faithful in their church and being a blessing by just helping out wherever they could.

For the first five years, all they did was to sit in the back pew at church, looking down at their feet because they felt so condemned. They knew they had made a big mistake, but they repented and eventually got their hearts right with God.

For the last five years, they have been working in church and being a strength to the Body of Christ. They have been tithing and giving, and God is blessing their business, their home and everything they have put their hands to.

Now their good reputation has been built back into the community and into the church. All their sins have been put behind them, and they have been proven worthy of God's calling.

Then what should that church do if he has been called and gifted of God? It should begin to utilize his ministerial gift by receiving him into the pulpit once again.

So, leadership is still available to those who have divorced and are remarried. But it will come to them again only after they have responded to God by repenting of their sin and seeking to follow Him. Before they can begin to walk in the ministerial qualifications that are listed in First Timothy, chapter 3, they have to take the time to straighten out the mess they had made in the past, fully surrendering themselves to God's will.

Quit Judging!

When a person again feels ready to enter into that responsibility of ministry, the church members must quit judging him according to his past experiences and be willing to receive from him as God's servant.

Some people in church may have a problem with a minister who has personally experienced divorce and remarriage. They will say: "I can't believe that person is being allowed to stand in our pulpit. I know for a fact that he was divorced and remarried ten years ago."

I would say to these people: "Just what have you been doing for the last ten years? That couple could have backslidden and left the church, but instead they came back here. Your piercing eyes were looking at them every Sunday, but they stood their ground. They have served God and loved Him, knowing they had made a big mistake. But God has forgiven them, and they have made the best out of their situation. They are moving on with God, and He is blessing them. Now you leave them alone! You should be praying for them instead of judging them for their past mistakes."

Maybe this is a new revelation to you. According to the Scriptures, that's exactly what Jesus did when He was here.

I guarantee you, people in Jesus' day had a hard time looking at the woman who once was an adulteress being called a virtuous woman the next day. But, you know, Jesus didn't have a problem with that. Neither did He have a problem with her being the one who ran to the Upper Room and told the disciples that He was alive. (John 20:18.) It seems to me that her sinful past didn't bother Him at all.

CONCLUSION

We have shown in this book what the Scriptures say about marriage, about divorce and about remarriage.

We have done what we could to try to untangle the mess that has developed through religious traditions and unscriptural ideas.

We have given you some spiritual principles to follow.

Now you must take the Word which you have been taught. Study it out. If it applies in any way to your past, then repent, if necessary, and let God restore your life. Let Him put His hand upon you so that you can enjoy a good covenant relationship with your spouse.

PRAYER

Heavenly Father, thank You for Your goodness and Your mercy. Your Word is life and health to those who find it, and Your truth sets people free.

Lord, thank You for laying a foundation from the Scriptures into the heart of the reader so that they might do what is pleasing in Your sight.

Father, let the person reading this book no longer be ruled by preconceived ideas placed in them from religious tradition and people's opinions from the past, but that they will choose to receive what the Word says. Your Word is the infallible Law, and it will work in their lives to produce the results You desire for them.

Many reading this book have been hurt; many have been in bondage; many have been defeated. So, touch every heart in need. Holy Spirit, minister healing and deliverance, in Jesus' name. Set the person reading this book free and bring them into a new walk of victory.

For those in the ministry who have gone through divorce, I pray that they will rebuild their relationship with You and gain a reputation of holiness in their lives. They must be willing to requalify themselves according to the Scripture. But, Lord, let them know that it's possible for them to be used by You again and possible to flow in Your blessings again.

Many have struggled with their remarriage because of the religious past and religious bondage. Many have doubted whether they were worthy to be used again in ministry. They have questioned whether You would bless them. They have even accepted a place of second best, because they didn't feel they could ever receive Your best again.

Father God, let them receive healing and know victory in their lives. Let new hope, new dreams and new visions come to pass for them.

Thank You, Father, for setting them free, for ministering to them Your truth that will bring freedom into their lives. In Jesus' Name. Amen.

ENDNOTES

Chapter 1

[1] *Webster's New World College Dictionary*, 3rd ed. (New York: MacMillian, 1996), s.v. "cleave."

Chapter 2

[1] Based on definition from James Strong, "Hebrew and Chaldee Dictionary" in *Strong's Exhaustive Concordance of the Bible* (Nashville: Abingdon, 1890), p. 87, entry #5828, from #5826, s.v. "help meet," Gen. 2:18 — "to surround, i.e. protect or aid: — help, succour" and definition from *The Amplified Bible New Testament* (AMP) copyright © 1954, 1958, 1987 by The Lockman Foundation, Gen. 2:18 — "one who is suitable, adapted, complementary."

Chapter 6

[1] Strong, "Hebrew and Chaldee Dictionary," p. 19, #898.

Chapter 8

[1] Strong, "Greek Dictionary of the New Testament," based on p. 49, #3429 from #3432, and "Hebrew and Chaldee Dictionary," p. 75, #5003.

[2] Ken Stewart D. Min., *Divorce and Remarriage* (Tulsa: Harrison House Publishers, 1984), p. 66.

Chapter 11

[1] Strong, "Greek Dictionary of the New Testament," p. 45, #3080.

Chapter 12

[1] Clark, "Matthew-Revelation" in *Clark's Commentary* (Nashville: Abingdon Press, 1824), p. 595.

ABOUT THE AUTHOR

Rev. Darrell Huffman entered into the full-time ministry in 1976. He graduated from Rhema Bible Training Center, in Tulsa, Oklahoma in 1978. For more than 18 years he has raised up churches in various parts of the United States. In July 1985, he started New Life Victory Center in Huntington, West Virginia, where he continues to pastor. A powerful and dynamic minister, Pastor Huffman ministers God's message with authority.

Pastor Huffman is also the Founder and President of Victory Ministries, Inc. & Victory Bible Training Center which are both based out of New Life Victory Center. Victory Ministries assists churches, evangelists and missionaries throughout the United States and in many foreign nations. Victory Bible Training Center is in its sixth year of classes with more than 500 students who graduated from the school. Along with these ministries, Victory of Faith Television and Radio Ministry is reaching out to multitudes of people daily in Huntington, The Tri-State and the East Coast.

God has used Pastor Huffman tremendously in helping the Body of Christ to understand who they are in Christ and the importance of knowing where they stand according to the Word of Almighty God. God has also anointed Pastor Huffman in ministering to those in need of healing through the laying on of hands and gifts of healings.

To contact the author, write:

Darrell Huffman
Huffman New Life Victory Center
1101 Cedar Crest Drive
Huntington, West Virginia 25705

Please include your prayer requests and comments when you write.

Copies of this book are available

from your local bookstore.

Harrison House

Tulsa, Oklahoma 74153

In Canada contact:

Word Alive

P. O. Box 670

Niverville, Manitoba

CANADA ROA 1EO